Toast

Toast

60 WAYS TO BUTTER YOUR BREAD & THEN SOME

JESSE ZIFF COOL

Photographs by DEBORAH JONES

CHRONICLE BOOKS
SAN FRANCISCO

Library of Congress Cataloging-in-Publication Data available.

ISBN 0-8118-3555-3

Manufactured in China.

Prop styling by Sara Slavin
Food styling by Sandra Cook
Designed by Carole Goodman / Blue Anchor Design
Typesetting by Bellina Shufro / Blue Anchor Design

Distributed in Canada by Raincoast Books
9050 Shaughnessy Street
Vancouver, British Columbia V6P 6E5

10 9 8 7 6 5 4 3 2 1

Chronicle Books LLC
85 Second Street
San Francisco, California 94105

www.chroniclebooks.com

ACKNOWLEDGMENTS

Thank you, Joshua, Yuko, and Masa Kun for keeping me in touch with the nurturing that comes through my family. I have needed them, and they are always there.

I wrote four books without an agent. The rest of the literary world thought I was crazy. I was simply waiting for the best. Thank you, Lisa Ekus, my agent, who takes care of me and my books with love, warmth, and deep care.

My dearests, Deborah Jones and Sandra Cook, created the images. They are the best, and I know it. Thanks for the crumbs; the irregularly torn pieces of toast; the hunky, chunky, not-perfect-looking toasty delights; intermingled with photos of my food looking elegant, gorgeous, and exquisite.

Thank you, Joey Altman, Michael Romano, Kay Smith, Patrick Roney, Beth Hensperger, Jonah Cool, and my sweet, sweet parents, June and Eddie Ziff, for inspiring great recipes. And Eric Mason, for continued words of motivation and friendship.

Sara Baer Sinnott and Dun Gifford, creators of Oldways Preservation and Trust Exchange, have taken me to all corners of the world, where more often than not, some kind of bread or toast was always within reach. Thank you, both, for your generosity and love.

I have never experienced a recipe tester as happy as Jean Cooper. She is the best, not only to work with but also as my confidante on girlie matters.

Bill LeBlond and Amy Treadwell at Chronicle accommodated my pushing deadlines. They also worked with me and made this book fun in the midst of utter turmoil in my life. Thanks also to Jan Hughes and Doug Ogan at Chronicle Books.

Finally, I wholeheartedly thank my staff in all three of my restaurants—they tolerate my mania in doing too much. This little book on toast was in process when New York was devastated on September 11. My mind and heart were elsewhere and in the midst, I had to run the businesses and write the book. My staff is family, and they are patient, supportive, and a loving team.

This book is dedicated to my youngest son, Jonah Cool. He is a good, healthy, and conscious eater as well as an extraordinary traveling mate. He continues to inspire, support, and lovingly yet firmly encourage me to be the best I can be. (Thanks, Lenny!)

Table of Contents

Introduction

There are four or five foods that I hunger for with frequency, anytime, anywhere. Toasted bread, in all forms, shapes, and doneness, tops my list. Like my mom, June, I find bread that is toasted to a perfect golden brown just as appealing as a few bites of the charred corners. Toast is basic and necessary. For me, it is soul food.

The wealth of ways to prepare and cook toast goes far beyond its global function as a morning repast. Toast appeals to me any time of the day. Morning toast with sweet butter, a toasted sandwich at lunch, and, at about 5 o'clock in the afternoon, a wedge of toasty bread with fruity olive oil and a glass of rustic Zinfandel hits the spot. Toasted bread as a platform for appetizers presents inexhaustible possibilities. And garlic toast is nearly always a welcome offering at the dinner table.

As often as I begin the day with toast, I end with it as well. More often than I like to admit, by the light of the refrigerator, you might find me snacking on a piece of toast slathered with cream cheese and blackberry jelly.

When it seems that the cupboard is bare, if I have a loaf of bread to toast, I can always find something to put on top of it. Warm and crunchy, it is the foundation for so much: dips, pâté, meats, fish, or poultry. Toast is a natural with tomatoes, roasted peppers, olives, garlic, and, of course, any kind of cheese.

Bread is the most nurturing food known to man. Straight out of the oven, it always makes me feel good. But, as I learned from my Italian grandfather, my Papa, bread does not have to be fresh from the baking pan to be enjoyed. Papa liked bread best when it was toasted. I used to sit on his lap, and he would tear off little pieces of what I called "Papa toast" and place them around the rim of the plate. We would dip the crusty pieces into the juices of whatever my grandmother had cooked. To this day, taking little pieces of toast, dipping, and then offering them to another is one of the most blessed acts of sharing food.

This is not a book on how to bake bread. It is designed to inspire you to use any bread toasted. It is about satisfyingly wonderful ways to create food from simple ingredients. Here you will rekindle the taste, the warmth, and the comfort of old favorites in dishes like "Egg in the Eye" with Extra Toasts for Dipping (page 17) and Sweet-Spice Cinnamon Toast (page 91). You will also venture into fresh and different ways to elevate toasted bread to a new position with recipes such as Toast with Wild Mushrooms, Truffle Oil, and Marsala (page 41), and Tarragon-Crusted Salmon with Olive-Caper Aioli on Toast (page 61). Toast will move to center stage, rather than being off to the side.

When you are caring for a loved one who is sick, toast often plays a vital role. For many, a bowl of chicken soup accompanied by a piece of toast is a welcome relief from misery. I've included family recipes like Grandma's Healing Toast (page 90). It is a simple recipe—toast with butter, sugar, and milk. A bowl of soothing ingredients put into the hands of another is a nurturing way to express love through food.

When a recipe calls for toasting bread, it is assumed that it is the bread of your choice, toasted on both sides in a standard upright toaster or toaster oven.

Breads can differ in style even though they are called by the same name. It is in the hands of the creator! Artisanal breads, which are handmade, are usually crusty and have a denser texture than commercially produced breads. They make great toast, with a more rustic texture and deeper, more interesting flavor. In my experience, there isn't a piece of bread, cut or torn, light or dark, thick or thin, that I would not consider toasting.

Breaking bread is a humbling way of sharing the bounty with others. Let us break bread, toast it, and give thanks for that which is simple and sustaining.

Toasting Techniques

Cutting Bread

A serrated bread knife is recommended for cutting bread and other baked goods. Although a sharp standard 8- or 10-inch chef's knife will work, a bread knife cuts through the loaf without tearing it.

Slicing versus Tearing Bread

Say what you like, toasted bread tastes different, depending on whether it's sliced or torn. It makes sense when you think about it. A sliced piece of bread toasts more evenly because the clean cut produces an even, flat surface. Putting smooth or chunky ingredients on top is a breeze. The mouth feel of knife-cut toast is more uniform.

Torn bread, on the other hand, has jagged surfaces and little ridges that give the toast extra crunch. Tearing also creates more crevices, little gullies, and rough places that catch, surround, make way for whatever is put on top of the toast. You have to drizzle or schmear on ingredients rather than spread them as you would with a sliced piece of toast. Torn toast is great for dipping and sopping up juices and is wonderful spread with soft, sensual cheeses.

You can cut bread into thick or thin slices. When toasted, thin slices are crunchier and can be more brittle. Thick-sliced toast is crusty on the outside and more flexible, supple, and soft in the middle. Try something a bit different by cutting the loaf into wedges.

Toasted over a Stovetop Flame

Yes, I toast bread on my commercial gas rangetop. Pierce a slice of bread with a long metal fork or skewer. Set the burner on medium-high and hold the bread over the flame, turning it until browned. Or carefully put the slice of bread directly over the grate that sits on top of the flame. Turn the bread with metal tongs until browned. This method also works well for toasting pita bread or fresh tortillas.

Bread Toasted over a Campfire

My favorite way to toast bread is over a campfire. The burning wood imparts a smoky flavor to the toast. And, as we all know, anything eaten out-of-doors, after an active day of hiking or swimming, somehow tastes better. It's easy to toast bread over a campfire. Think about all those times you toasted marshmallows. The flame has to be medium-high or the food will burn (remember those torched marshmallows). Put the bread on a grill or use a metal toasting tool, available in many camping supply stores. As a last resort, poke a stick through the bread and toast it over the flame. Be sure to turn the bread frequently.

Bread Toasted over a Barbecue Grill

Use medium-hot coals when making toast over an outdoor barbecue. Even a gas grill will impart a smoked flavor, though not as intense as when using mesquite charcoal. Put the bread on the grate, turning often, until browned. Brushing the bread first with olive oil or butter adds crispness, prevents the bread from sticking, and gives the toast irresistible flavor.

Toasting Appliances

Traditional Upright Toaster

You'll find a wide range of types and prices of toasters on the market today. For longevity, buy a sturdy, heavy toaster. Other factors to consider are

SIZE, SHAPE, AND ACCESS IN YOUR KITCHEN: Before making your purchase, think about where you are going to plug the toaster into the wall so it will be easily accessible.

NUMBER OF SLOTS: Buy a toaster with four or more slots only if you are going to use them. Otherwise it is a waste of space and energy to have such a big toaster.

SIZE OF SLOTS: Larger slots are more versatile. Besides toasting regular or thick slices of bread, you can toast bagels as well as frozen turnovers, empanadas, calzones, and other pastries.

CONTROL SETTINGS: Buy a toaster with reliable darkness settings so you can trust that it will toast the bread to your liking.

CLEANING: How easy is it to clean the toaster and remove the crumbs?

Toaster Oven

This versatile, practical appliance is my first choice for making any kind of toast. You can use it for toasting bread of any size or thickness as well as for broiling and baking small quantities of food. It is energy efficient and heats up faster than a standard oven.

Sandwich Toasting Iron

Using a toasting iron produces sealed toasted sandwiches, usually with a clam-shaped impression on the outside. Lightly butter or oil the inside surface of the iron and put the sandwich inside. Clamp the iron together and, using a knife, cut off any crusts that don't fit inside. Do not overfill. Do not wash the inside of the iron; instead, after each use, wipe it clean with a paper towel. After a number of uses, the iron should be seasoned, so you can use less butter or oil on the iron.

Panini Grill

This appliance is fantastic for grilling sandwiches and toasting bread. We use them in my restaurant, jZcool Eatery and Catering Company, where we grill dozens of premade sandwiches daily. Small versions are sold in most good cookware shops but often require higher voltage than is available in most home kitchens. You can cook a variety of other foods besides sandwiches in a panini grill. It is great for making French toast and for warming up and crisping the outsides of croissants, breakfast rolls, and bagels. Do not wash the inside of the grill; instead, after each use, brush away crumbs or other food. Lightly oil the surfaces if sticking occurs.

Cast-Iron Skillet

I like iron skillets because they conduct heat evenly. Because my skillets are well seasoned, I use very little fat or oil. Sometimes, rather than using an upright toaster or a toaster oven, I heat an iron skillet over high heat and then put lightly buttered bread in the skillet to toast.

Waffle Iron

Waffle irons come in a wide variety of styles. I have an old-fashioned one that is designed for use on a gas stovetop, although electric waffle irons are easier to control. If the waffle iron surface is not nonstick, be sure to generously oil or butter the grids before each use. Waffle irons are wonderful for toasting sandwiches. You can also use a waffle iron to make French toast. Use your favorite recipe or try the Waffle-Iron Orange French Toast (page 29). The grids create a crisp surface on the toast.

Bagel Toaster

The main advantage of a bagel toaster is that it toasts only one side. The toasting slots are bigger to accommodate thick bagels as well as oversize English muffins, hand-cut bread, and other odd-sized bread products that you want to toast on one side.

Breakfast

Toast, all by itself or perhaps spread with a little butter and jam, often comes to mind as I crawl out of bed in the morning. I stumble into the kitchen and brew a cup of English breakfast tea with lots of milk and a little honey while the toaster is browning a slice of bread. I lean against the counter, sipping my tea and waiting with anticipation of dunking the toast into my mug and beginning the day with humble sustenance.

But morning toast goes beyond topping it with butter and jam. I have won many a heart by starting someone's day with a toasted sandwich, such as the Summer Breakfast Sandwich with Tomatoes, Avocado, and Cheddar Cheese (page 21). My youngest son, Jonah, always loved the unusual concoction of baked beans on toast. One morning I cooked French toast in a waffle iron and the kids went wild. No one around my house ever tires of the satisfyingly all-American breakfast of a perfectly fried egg (gathered from my chicken coop) accompanied by a pile of crispy potatoes and warm, crusty toast for dipping into the golden yolks.

The possibilities for imaginative breakfast toast are endless, as you will discover in these recipes.

"Egg in the Eye" with Extra Toasts for Dipping

OK, so a book about toast is going to include lots of family favorites. Both of my kids, who are grown and cooking for themselves now, never tired of this dish. In truth, the best part was always the little piece of toast that came from the cutout circle in the middle of the bread, where the yolk peeks through. Jonah, my youngest, was very happy when I buttered an extra slice of bread, cut it into little pieces, and toasted it, so he could have more crispy toast for dipping in the yolk. This recipe calls for only 1 egg per person. You can cut a larger hole in each bread slice and cook 2 eggs inside.

Using a knife or a 2-inch round cookie cutter, cut a circle out of the center of 4 of the bread slices. Cut the crusts off the other 2 slices and cut each into 4 pieces.

Choose 1 large or 2 medium heavy-bottomed skillets that will hold all the bread, including the extra toasts. Over medium heat, melt 2 tablespoons of the butter in the pan(s). Place the bread with the holes in the pan(s) and crack 1 egg into each hole. Place the little pieces of bread, including the circles, around the slices. Using a spatula, lightly push down on all of the bread so it absorbs the butter.

Cover and cook for about 3 minutes. Uncover and add the remaining 2 tablespoons butter to the outside edges of the pan(s) to melt it. Using a spatula, turn the little pieces of bread and the circles over, tilting the pan slightly so the butter runs underneath the bread. Brown the other side of the bread and cook until the yolks are done to your liking, about 5 minutes for medium-cooked yolks. If the toasts are browned before the eggs are cooked, remove them and set aside. Season with salt and pepper to taste.

6 BREAD SLICES

4 TABLESPOONS UNSALTED BUTTER AT ROOM TEMPERATURE

4 EGGS

SALT AND FRESHLY GROUND PEPPER

SERVES 4

BREAD SUGGESTIONS
White, wheat, Italian, sourdough, potato, English muffins.

Jonah's Beans and Toast

Beans and toast are a great way to get protein into children before they run off to school in the morning. Jonah is in college now, but he used to make baked bean and ketchup sandwiches to devour on his way to school.

Any kind of cooked beans, such as pinto or black beans, can be used, but for this recipe, canned baked beans work best because you need the juices to moisten the toast. If you cook your own beans, reserve some of the cooking liquid and season it with extra onion, thyme, and ketchup. Glorify this humble dish by topping it with green onions, or grilled red onions, grated Cheddar cheese, or even sour cream.

In a medium saucepan over medium heat, combine the beans and their juices, onion, thyme, and $1/4$ cup of the ketchup and simmer for about 5 minutes.

Meanwhile, in a medium skillet, melt 1 tablespoon of the butter. Crack the eggs into the pan, cover, and cook for about 4 minutes for medium-cooked yolks.

Toast the bread and spread the remaining 2 tablespoons butter on the slices. Place 2 slices, buttered-side up and overlapping slightly, on each of 4 plates. Using a spatula, transfer 1 egg onto each of 2 slices of toast. Spoon the beans over the eggs and toast. Top with the remaining $1/4$ cup ketchup, dividing evenly. Pass hot sauce at the table, if using.

SERVES 4

2 CANS (EACH 16 OUNCES) BAKED BEANS WITH JUICES, OR 4 CUPS COOKED BEANS, COOKING LIQUID RESERVED

2 TABLESPOONS GRATED YELLOW ONION

2 TABLESPOONS CHOPPED FRESH THYME

$1/2$ CUP KETCHUP

3 TABLESPOONS UNSALTED BUTTER

4 EGGS

8 BREAD SLICES

HOT SAUCE FOR SERVING (OPTIONAL)

BREAD SUGGESTIONS
Whole grain, country white, sourdough, English muffins, corn bread, crumpets.

Toast with Eggs, Asparagus, and Lemon-Chive Butter

6 TABLESPOONS UNSALTED BUTTER AT ROOM TEMPERATURE

1 SMALL TOMATO, SEEDED AND FINELY CHOPPED

1/4 CUP CHOPPED FRESH CHIVES, PLUS MORE FOR GARNISHING

2 TABLESPOONS FRESH LEMON JUICE

1/4 TEASPOON SWEET PAPRIKA

1/2 TEASPOON SALT

PINCH OF CAYENNE PEPPER

8 BREAD SLICES

8 EGGS

1 POUND ASPARAGUS

Many of us love hollandaise sauce but hesitate to eat it because of the fat content. I've found a way to enjoy the sensual quality of the sauce minus some of the fat—by letting egg yolks and butter drip into toast. The more butter you use, the more it tastes and has the mouth feel of real hollandaise sauce.

Preheat the broiler. In a small bowl, combine the butter, tomato, the 1/4 cup chives, lemon juice, paprika, salt, and cayenne. Spread a thin layer of the seasoned butter on the bread. Place the bread on a baking sheet and broil for 3 to 4 minutes, or until browned.

Meanwhile, cook the eggs. For poached eggs, in a medium saucepan over medium heat, bring 1 1/2 quarts salted water to a simmer. Crack the eggs into the water. Simmer for 3 minutes. For fried eggs, in a medium skillet over medium heat, melt 1 tablespoon of the seasoned butter, crack the eggs into the pan, cover, and cook for about 3 minutes, leaving the yolks runny.

Cut or break off the bottom of the asparagus spears. Place in a steamer basket over a pot of boiling water. Steam for 3 to 5 minutes, or until tender.

Place 2 slices of toast on each of 4 plates. Top each with one-fourth of the asparagus and then with 2 eggs. Spoon about 2 teaspoons of the seasoned butter over each serving. Garnish with chives.

SERVES 4

MAKE-AHEAD TIP To save time in the morning, make the seasoned butter the night before and spread it on the bread. Store in an airtight container and refrigerate. In the morning, toast the bread as directed.

BREAD SUGGESTIONS
White, whole grain, baguette, sourdough, English muffins, crumpets.

Summer Breakfast Sandwich with Tomatoes, Avocado, and Cheddar Cheese

2 TABLESPOONS EXTRA-VIRGIN OLIVE OIL

1 LARGE TOMATO, CUT INTO 4 SLICES

SALT AND FRESHLY GROUND PEPPER

4 EGGS

1 GREEN ONION (BOTH WHITE AND GREEN PARTS), THINLY SLICED

1 TABLESPOON CHOPPED FRESH THYME

4 OUNCES CHEDDAR CHEESE, GRATED

1 AVOCADO, PITTED, PEELED, AND THINLY SLICED

8 BREAD SLICES OR 4 ENGLISH MUFFINS

2 TABLESPOONS GRATED PARMIGIANO-REGGIANO CHEESE

As with many recipes in this book, you can hard-cook the egg yolks or leave them slightly runny, letting them ooze into the crusty toast. Any salty meat, such as ham, bacon, prosciutto, or smoked turkey, is wonderful in these sandwiches. Place thin slices of meat on the bottom of the pan and top with the tomato slices.

In a large sauté pan over medium heat, warm the olive oil. Add the tomato slices and season with salt and pepper to taste. Crack 1 egg on top of each tomato slice. It's OK if some of the egg runs off the tomato. Sprinkle the green onion, thyme, and Cheddar cheese on top of the eggs. Cover and cook for 4 to 5 minutes, or until done to your liking. Top the eggs with the avocado slices.

Toast the bread. Place 1 slice on each of 4 plates. Using a spatula, transfer 1 tomato slice and 1 egg onto each slice. Sprinkle with the Parmigiano-Reggiano cheese and then top each with another slice of toast. Cut the sandwiches in half and serve.

SERVES 4

BREAD SUGGESTIONS
English muffins, sourdough, sweet white, whole grain, rosemary, olive, cheese, black pepper.

Toast with Scrambled Eggs, Jam, and Cheddar Cheese

This recipe was inspired by my Jewish past. When I was a child, we ate Cheddar cheese and jelly omelettes. When you think about it, the dish is almost like a fruit crepe but is quicker and heartier. The classic combination of fruit and cheese is tucked inside fluffy eggs instead of a crepe. Sometimes I fold the jam into the eggs just before sprinkling on the cheese, which warms up the jam a bit.

In a medium bowl, whisk together the eggs, milk, and green onions. Season with salt and pepper to taste.

In a medium sauté pan over medium heat, melt 2 tablespoons of the butter. Add the egg mixture. Using a large spoon or rubber spatula, push the eggs from the outside of the pan, where they cook the fastest, toward the center, turning occasionally, until they are cooked halfway. Sprinkle the cheese over the eggs. Cover and reduce the heat to low. Let the cheese melt and the eggs cook for about 3 minutes, or until done to your liking.

Meanwhile, toast the bread. Spread the remaining 2 tablespoons butter and the jam on the slices. Place 1 slice on each of 4 plates. Spoon the scrambled eggs on top of the toast and sprinkle with the parsley.

SERVES 4

8 EGGS

4 TABLESPOONS MILK

2 GREEN ONIONS (BOTH WHITE AND GREEN PARTS), CHOPPED

SALT AND FRESHLY GROUND PEPPER

4 TABLESPOONS UNSALTED BUTTER

6 OUNCES CHEDDAR CHEESE, GRATED

4 BREAD SLICES

4 TABLESPOONS GRAPE OR BLACKBERRY JAM, OR AS NEEDED

2 TABLESPOONS CHOPPED FRESH FLAT-LEAF PARSLEY

BREAD SUGGESTIONS
Rye, white, sourdough, whole grain, English muffins, pugliese, ciabatta.

Toast with Green Eggs and Ham

1 BUNCH SPINACH (ABOUT 1 POUND), STEMMED AND WASHED

1 CLOVE GARLIC

1 CUP CHOPPED FRESH BASIL

2 TABLESPOONS OLIVE OIL

8 EGGS, BEATEN

SALT AND FRESHLY GROUND PEPPER

2 TABLESPOONS UNSALTED BUTTER

8 OUNCES HAM, THINLY SLICED

4 OUNCES CHEDDAR CHEESE, GRATED

6 BREAD SLICES

2 GREEN ONIONS (BOTH WHITE AND GREEN PARTS), CHOPPED

Green Eggs and Ham, the children's book by Dr. Seuss, inspired this dish. It's a great way to get kids to eat spinach.

Place spinach in a steamer basket above simmering water. Cover and steam for 2 minutes. Remove and drain off excess water. When the spinach is cool enough to handle, using your hands, squeeze out most of the liquid. Put the spinach, garlic, basil, and olive oil in a food processor or blender and purée. Add a small amount of water if needed.

Transfer the spinach mixture to a medium bowl and add the eggs. Season with salt and pepper to taste.

In a medium sauté pan over medium heat, melt the butter. Add the ham and cook, stirring occasionally, for 2 minutes. Add the egg-spinach mixture. Using a large spoon or rubber spatula, push the eggs from the outside of the pan, where they cook the fastest, toward the center, turning occasionally, until they are cooked, about 4 minutes, or until done to your liking. Turn off the heat. Sprinkle the cheese over the eggs and cover the pan.

Meanwhile, toast the bread. Cut the slices in half and arrange 3 halves on each of 4 plates. Spoon one-fourth of the green eggs and ham onto each plate. Sprinkle with the green onions.

SERVES 4

MAKE-AHEAD TIP
So you can prepare breakfast quickly in the morning, cook the spinach and make the spinach purée the night before. Slice the ham, grate the cheese, and store it all in the refrigerator.

BREAD SUGGESTIONS
Rye, whole grain, white, sourdough, raisin, potato, herb, olive.

Autumn Breakfast Sandwich with Ratatouille, Prosciutto, and Parmigiano-Reggiano

8 HAND-CUT BREAD SLICES,
(EACH 1 INCH THICK)

2 TO 3 TABLESPOONS EXTRA-VIRGIN OLIVE OIL

2 CLOVES GARLIC, HALVED

6 CUPS RATATOUILLE (PAGE 26)

3-OUNCE WEDGE OF PARMIGIANO-REGGIANO CHEESE

1/4 POUND THINLY SLICED PROSCIUTTO, CUT INTO 1/4-INCH STRIPS

BREAD SUGGESTIONS
Baguette, Italian, sourdough, country wheat, focaccia, ciabatta, pugliese.

It was late September. The night before, I had cooked up a big batch of ratatouille, which we had for dinner with an oven-roasted organic chicken. And, though it was good, we knew that this classic stew was going to taste even better as leftovers.

The next morning, my buddy Eric stopped by, and he never turns down breakfast. He knows I will open the refrigerator and come up with something. I like unusual combinations for breakfast, especially savory ones. I happened to have a little prosciutto, and I knew the ratatouille would be great with it, especially toasted in a sandwich along with a little cheese. He left a satisfied man.

The ratatouille recipe makes more than what you'll need for the sandwiches. Leftovers can be frozen in small sealable plastic bags for later use. It keeps for 2 months in the freezer.

Preheat the broiler of the oven or toaster oven.

Brush the bread generously with the olive oil and then rub with the garlic. Place the bread on a baking sheet and broil for about 4 minutes, or until browned.

Meanwhile, in a medium saucepan over medium heat, warm the ratatouille for 5 to 7 minutes. Place 2 slices of toast on each of 4 plates. Spoon the ratatouille on top of the toast. Using a vegetable peeler, peel a generous amount of the cheese onto the ratatouille. Rustically arrange the prosciutto on top.

SERVES 4

In a medium heavy-bottomed sauté pan over medium heat, warm the olive oil and garlic. Add the eggplant, bell pepper, onion, zucchini, tomato, and broth. Cover and cook, stirring occasionally, for about 30 minutes, or until the vegetables are very soft. Add the capers and basil and cook, uncovered, for 5 minutes longer. Season with salt and pepper to taste.

Ratatouille

1/4 CUP OLIVE OIL

2 CLOVES GARLIC, MINCED

1 MEDIUM GLOBE EGGPLANT, CUT INTO
1/2-INCH CUBES

1 MEDIUM RED BELL PEPPER, SEEDED,
DERIBBED, AND CUT INTO 1/2-INCH PIECES

1 MEDIUM ONION, CUT INTO 1/2-INCH PIECES

1 MEDIUM ZUCCHINI, CUT INTO 1-INCH PIECES

1 VERY RIPE LARGE TOMATO, SEEDED AND CUT
INTO 1/2-INCH PIECES

1 CUP CHICKEN BROTH OR WATER

1 1/2 TABLESPOONS CAPERS

1/2 CUP CHOPPED FRESH BASIL

SALT AND FRESHLY GROUND PEPPER

Toast with Lox and Caper-Dill Cream Cheese

8 OUNCES CREAM CHEESE AT ROOM TEMPERATURE, OR WHIPPED SOFT CREAM CHEESE

2 TABLESPOONS CHOPPED FRESH DILL

1 GREEN ONION (BOTH WHITE AND GREEN PARTS), VERY THINLY SLICED

1 TABLESPOON CAPERS

1 TEASPOON LEMON ZEST

1/3 POUND LOX, THINLY SLICED

1 LARGE TOMATO, SEEDED AND COARSELY CHOPPED

1/2 SMALL RED ONION, FINELY CHOPPED

1/2 CUCUMBER, PEELED, SEEDED, AND COARSELY CHOPPED

8 BREAD SLICES (EACH 1/4 TO 1/2 INCH THICK)

Toasted bagels are a natural for this traditional Jewish-style brunch dish. But I like thick slices of toasted rye or challah bread as much as bagels. I break the toast into pieces and top them with a large pinch of each of the ingredients. I have eaten my share of traditionally assembled bagels and lox but, for some reason, I think this version tastes better.

In a medium bowl, combine the cream cheese, dill, green onion, capers, and lemon zest. On a large platter, arrange the lox along with mounds of the tomato, red onion, and cucumber.

Toast the bread and break into large pieces. Spread the pieces with the caper-dill cream cheese. Top each with some of the lox. Then rustically pile the tomato, red onion, and cucumber on top.

SERVES 4 TO 6

MAKE-AHEAD TIP
The caper-dill cream cheese can be made in advance and refrigerated in an airtight container for up to 1 week.

BREAD SUGGESTIONS
Rye, challah, potato, brioche, country white, bagels, English muffins.

Waffle-Iron Orange French Toast

3 EGGS

1 CUP MILK

1/2 CUP FRESH ORANGE JUICE

3 TABLESPOONS SUGAR

1/2 TEASPOON VANILLA EXTRACT

1/2 TEASPOON GROUND CINNAMON

1 TABLESPOON FINELY GRATED ORANGE ZEST
(PREFERABLY ORGANIC)

8 BREAD SLICES (EACH 3/4 INCH THICK)

2 TABLESPOONS UNSALTED BUTTER
AT ROOM TEMPERATURE, IF NEEDED

If you have never used a waffle iron for anything besides making waffles, you are missing out on a great way to cook French toast. The metal ridges that create a crusty exterior and moist interior on waffles produce similar results with French toast. For extra-moist French toast, soak the bread in the egg-milk mixture overnight in the refrigerator. Serve with maple syrup, jam, fresh fruit, nuts, yogurt, or sour cream.

Preheat the waffle iron on medium.

In a pie plate or shallow bowl, using a whisk or fork, beat together the eggs, milk, orange juice, sugar, vanilla, cinnamon, and orange zest. Soak the bread slices in the egg-milk mixture for at least 15 seconds per side. The longer the bread is soaked, the moister the French toast. Cook immediately or refrigerate until ready to use.

If using a regular waffle iron, brush it lightly with the butter. If it is nonstick, you don't need the butter. Place the bread in the waffle iron (how many slices you can cook at a time depends upon your waffle iron). Close the iron and, using a sharp knife, cut off any bread that extends beyond the edge of the iron. Cook for about 5 minutes, or until the bread is toasted on the outside.

SERVES 4

BREAD SUGGESTIONS
White, sourdough, brioche, raisin, cinnamon, challah, Cheddar cheese.

Toast with Oven-Roasted Tomatoes, Basil, and Poached Eggs

2 LARGE TOMATOES, EACH CUT INTO 4 SLICES

2 CLOVES GARLIC, MINCED

3 TABLESPOONS EXTRA-VIRGIN OLIVE OIL

$1^{1}/_{2}$ CUPS FRESH BASIL, COARSELY CHOPPED

SALT AND FRESHLY GROUND PEPPER

1 TABLESPOON CIDER VINEGAR

4 EGGS

4 HAND-CUT BREAD SLICES (EACH ABOUT
$1/_{2}$ INCH THICK)

2 GREEN ONIONS (BOTH WHITE AND GREEN
PARTS), THINLY SLICED

This dish is best when tomatoes are at their prime—juicy, ripe, and full of flavor. When tomatoes are not in season, use top-quality canned ones. Drain off the juices and roast as directed for fresh ones.

Preheat the oven to 400 degrees F.

In a medium bowl, toss the tomatoes with the garlic, olive oil, and 1 cup of the basil. Place the tomatoes on a baking sheet and season with salt and pepper to taste. Bake for 20 minutes, or until the tomatoes are slightly shriveled and beginning to brown.

Turn off the oven but leave the tomatoes inside to stay warm.

In a medium saucepan over medium heat, combine the vinegar with about 4 cups water. Bring to a simmer. Crack the eggs into the water. Simmer for about 3 minutes for soft-cooked, 5 minutes for medium, and 7 minutes for well-cooked eggs.

Toast the bread. Place 1 slice on each of 4 plates. Using a large spoon, scoop 2 tomato slices and any juices onto each slice of toast. Sprinkle green onions over the tomatoes.

Using a slotted spoon, transfer 1 poached egg onto each of 2 tomato slices. Season with salt and pepper to taste and sprinkle the remaining $1/_{2}$ cup basil over all.

SERVES 4

MAKE-AHEAD TIP
The tomatoes can be roasted ahead of time. Store them along with their juices in the refrigerator for up to 2 days. Rewarm the tomatoes and juices for a few minutes before serving.

BREAD SUGGESTIONS
Country white, Italian, sourdough, rosemary, olive, whole grain, ciabatta.

Winter Breakfast Sandwich with Maple Syrup, Toasted Walnuts, and Cream Cheese

Bread isn't the only food that tastes great when toasted. Toasting brings out the oils and deepens the flavor of nuts. This toasted treat is delicious for breakfast and is also a welcome pleasure in the middle of the afternoon, with a cup of Darjeeling tea or dark, rich coffee.

Preheat the toaster oven to 350 degrees F.

Put the walnuts on a baking tray and toast for 5 minutes. Let cool to room temperature.

In a medium bowl, combine the cream cheese, the 3 tablespoons maple syrup, the cinnamon, nutmeg, and vanilla and stir to blend.

Toast the bread. Spread one-fourth of the cream cheese mixture on each of 4 slices and sprinkle with the walnuts. Drizzle with a little maple syrup. Top each with a slice of plain toast. Cut each into 2, 4, or even 6 pieces (for tiny bite-sized tea sandwiches).

SERVES 4 TO 6

2/3 CUP (ABOUT 3 OUNCES) COARSELY CHOPPED WALNUTS

8 OUNCES CREAM CHEESE AT ROOM TEMPERATURE

3 TABLESPOONS REAL MAPLE SYRUP, PLUS MORE FOR GARNISHING

1/4 TEASPOON GROUND CINNAMON

PINCH OF FRESHLY GRATED NUTMEG

1/2 TEASPOON VANILLA EXTRACT

8 BREAD SLICES

MAKE-AHEAD TIP
Prepare the cream cheese mixture the night before and refrigerate it. The next morning, let it soften at room temperature.

BREAD SUGGESTIONS
Raisin, oat, wheat, whole grain, bagels, white.

Appetizers

The most popular appetizers prepared by my catering company are the
ones that have something gloriously delicious piled on top of toast. The bread can be sliced thick or thin, depending on how
crunchy or sturdy the toasty base needs to be to support the topping. Sometimes the toast is called bruschetta, which is grilled
bread that serves as a platform for juicy, unctuous toppings like Toast with Tomatoes, Anchovies, and Capers (page 46).
Thinner toasts, known as crostini, are great for a schmear of chopped chicken liver (I've included my mom's recipe in this
chapter, page 45). The toppings can be neatly spread on the toasts using a knife or slid off a spoon, so they are more rustic
in style. Or, for a buffet, pile the topping in the middle of a platter and surround it with little crusty toasts.

Appetizer toasts are ideal for a light lunch or afternoon tea. To create a simple but impressive meal, toss a big green salad
and serve it next to a platter of Toast with Smoked Chicken, Strawberries, and Chives (page 49) or Little Toasts with Smoked
Whitefish and Apples (page 47).

The truth is, you can put almost anything on small pieces of toast and serve it as an appetizer. That's how I got the idea for
Little Meatballs on Garlic Toast (page 50)—I used leftovers, and wowed unexpected guests.

In other words, pick up that piece of toast and let your imagination go. Now and then, give the butter and jam a rest.

Spanish Tomato Toast

My friend Joey Altman first had this wonderful appetizer when he was traveling in Spain. What makes this tomato feast different is that you smoosh half of a tomato, pushing it into the toast to create a thick, rich sauce. The quality of the ingredients—the bread, the olive oil, and especially the tomatoes—is the key to the appetizer's success. Consider using tomatoes in a range of colors. You could mash a combination of golden, purple, red, and even ripe green ones on top to create a gorgeous appetizer.

Preheat the broiler.

Generously brush the bread with some of the olive oil, then rub with the garlic. Place the bread on a baking sheet and broil for about 4 minutes, or until browned.

Remove the stems and any bruises from the tomatoes. Cut them in half horizontally and squeeze out the seeds. Using your hand, rub the cut side of a tomato half over a slice of toast, mashing the tomato and lightly pushing the juices and flesh into the toast. When the tomato is broken down, mound it evenly on the toast. Season generously with salt and pepper to taste. Drizzle with olive oil. Repeat with the remaining tomatoes and toast. Arrange on a serving platter.

SERVES 4 TO 6

8 CRUSTY BREAD SLICES (EACH ABOUT 3/4 INCH THICK)

1/2 CUP EXTRA-VIRGIN OLIVE OIL

2 CLOVES GARLIC, PEELED

4 VERY RIPE, JUICY MEDIUM TOMATOES

SALT AND FRESHLY GROUND PEPPER

BREAD SUGGESTIONS
Ciabatta, pugliese, any crusty country bread.

Toast with Roasted Red Bell Peppers

4 LARGE RED BELL PEPPERS (ABOUT
1¹/₂ POUNDS TOTAL)

¹/₂ CUP EXTRA-VIRGIN OLIVE OIL

4 CLOVES GARLIC, FINELY CHOPPED

2 TABLESPOONS BALSAMIC VINEGAR

1 CUP MINCED FRESH BASIL

SALT AND FRESHLY GROUND PEPPER

1 LOAF FLAT ITALIAN BREAD

³/₄ CUP (2 OUNCES) GRATED
PECORINO CHEESE

BREAD SUGGESTIONS:
Italian, herb, olive, white,
pugliese, chapati, sourdough.

Simple and easy, roasted bell peppers on toasted bread are always an appealing appetizer. This rendition celebrates the sweet seductive qualities of peppers at their peak, from mid-August through late autumn. Besides the classic bells, you'll find other interesting and tasty peppers at farmers' markets. One of my favorites is the long, sweet, and wonderfully flavored Gypsy pepper. For an extra kick, use a few spicy red chiles along with the sweet peppers. To make this toast more like a pizza, top the bread with fresh mozzarella cheese before broiling.

Preheat the broiler.

Place the bell peppers on a baking sheet and broil for about 15 minutes, or until the skins are charred all over and the flesh is soft. Transfer the peppers to a pan and cover with a lid. Do not turn off the broiler. Let the peppers stand for 15 minutes. Remove them from the pan, reserving the juices. Using your hands, slip off the charred skin and remove the seeds. Strain the juices through a fine-mesh sieve and set aside.

Tear the peppers into strips. Put them in a bowl along with ¹/4 cup of the olive oil, the garlic, vinegar, ¹/2 cup of the basil, and the reserved pepper juices. Season with salt and pepper to taste.

Cut the bread in half horizontally. Brush the cut sides with the remaining ¹/4 cup olive oil and sprinkle with the cheese. Place on a baking sheet and broil for about 3 to 4 minutes, or until lightly browned.

Spread the peppers and juices on the bread. Cut into slices and season with pepper to taste. Arrange on a serving platter and sprinkle with the remaining basil.

SERVES 4 TO 6

Toasted Pita Bread with Greek White Bean Spread

1/3 CUP EXTRA-VIRGIN OLIVE OIL

2 TABLESPOONS CHOPPED RED ONION

2 CLOVES GARLIC, MINCED

1 CAN (15 OUNCES) WHITE BEANS, OR
1 1/2 CUPS OF COOKED BEANS, DRAINED
AND JUICES RESERVED

1/2 CUP FINELY CHOPPED TOMATO, PLUS
MORE FOR GARNISHING

1/2 CUP FINELY CHOPPED CUCUMBER, PLUS
MORE FOR GARNISHING

3 TABLESPOONS CHOPPED FRESH FLAT-LEAF
PARSLEY, PLUS MORE FOR GARNISHING

3 TABLESPOONS CHOPPED FRESH MINT

2 TABLESPOONS FRESH LEMON JUICE

SALT AND FRESHLY GROUND PEPPER

4 TO 6 PITA BREAD ROUNDS, TOASTED

If you have a gas stove, toast the pita bread over the open flame. Use metal tongs to hold the bread and turn it until lightly browned. Or, toast the pita in a toaster oven for a few minutes. I have also used a standard upright toaster on the light setting, turning the rounds halfway through so all sides get toasted. This dish also makes an excellent accompaniment to grilled fish or chicken.

In a medium sauté pan over medium heat, warm 3 tablespoons of the olive oil. Add the onion and garlic and cook for 5 minutes, or until soft. Add the beans and 1/4 cup of the reserved juices. Reduce the heat to low, cover, and simmer for 5 minutes. Uncover and, using a fork, mash the beans. Transfer to a medium bowl and let cool to room temperature.

Add the 1/2 cup tomato, 1/2 cup cucumber, 3 tablespoons parsley, the mint, lemon juice, and half the remaining olive oil to the beans and stir to mix. If needed, add more bean juice to make the mixture spreadable. Season with salt and pepper to taste.

Mound the bean spread on a serving platter and drizzle with the remaining olive oil. Cut or tear the pita bread into bite-sized pieces and arrange them next to the bean spread. Garnish with chopped tomato, cucumber, and parsley.

SERVES 6

BREAD SUGGESTIONS
Whole-wheat or white pita, whole grain, white, herb, olive.

Toast with Cipollini Onions, Port, and Stilton Cheese

8 MEDIUM CIPOLLINI ONIONS, PEELED

1 CUP CHICKEN OR VEGETABLE BROTH, PLUS
MORE AS NEEDED

2 TABLESPOONS EXTRA-VIRGIN OLIVE OIL

1 CUP RUBY PORT

3 FRESH THYME SPRIGS

PINCH OF CAYENNE PEPPER (OPTIONAL)

8 BAGUETTE SLICES, EACH LARGE ENOUGH
TO HOLD A WHOLE CIPOLLINI ONION

6 OUNCES STILTON CHEESE

1 TABLESPOON CHOPPED FRESH FLAT-LEAF
PARSLEY

A few years ago, my dear friend Michael Romano cooked dinner for me at his house in the Hamptons. One of the dishes was cipollini onions in red wine with butter and herbs. I have used this recipe many times, substituting port for the wine. It is perfect with the pungent, salty Stilton cheese. If you can't handle the "bigness" of Stilton, substitute a milder blue-veined cheese, such as Blue Costello or Roquefort.

In a medium saucepan over medium heat, combine the onions, broth, olive oil, port, thyme, and cayenne pepper, if using. Simmer, stirring occasionally, for 15 minutes, or until the onions are soft but still hold their shape. Add more broth if necessary. Using a slotted spoon, transfer the onions to a bowl. Simmer the juices for 5 minutes, or until reduced to a light syrup. Remove the thyme sprigs and discard.

Toast the bread. Spread a small amount of the Stilton on each slice, and spoon an onion and some juices on top. Garnish with the parsley and arrange on a serving platter.

SERVES 4

BREAD SUGGESTIONS
Seeded or plain baguette,
brioche, country white,
wheat.

Toast with Wild Mushrooms, Truffle Oil, and Marsala

2 TABLESPOONS OLIVE OIL

2 MEDIUM LEEKS (TOUGH GREEN LEAVES REMOVED), SLICED AND THOROUGHLY WASHED

4 CLOVES GARLIC; 3 MINCED, 1 HALVED

1 POUND CHANTERELLES, PORCINI, MORELS, OR OTHER WILD MUSHROOMS, THOROUGHLY CLEANED AND COARSELY CHOPPED

1 TABLESPOON CHOPPED FRESH THYME

1/4 CUP MARSALA WINE

SALT AND FRESHLY GROUND PEPPER

2 TABLESPOONS UNSALTED BUTTER, AT ROOM TEMPERATURE

1 TABLESPOON TRUFFLE OIL

6 CRUSTY BREAD SLICES (EACH 1/2 INCH THICK)

If you want to "wow" your guests with an appetizer that seems exotic, this is it. You can find truffle oil in gourmet grocery stores. Buy a small bottle because a little truffle oil goes a long way. It keeps well in the refrigerator and is wonderful drizzled over pasta or roasted chicken. If you can't find wild mushrooms, shiitakes will work just fine. This recipe is also delicious with goat cheese. After spooning the mushrooms on the toasts, crumble a bit of goat cheese on top.

In a medium sauté pan over medium heat, warm the olive oil. Add the leeks and cook, stirring occasionally, for about 10 minutes, or until soft. Add the minced garlic, mushrooms, and thyme and cook for about 5 minutes. Increase the heat to high, add the Marsala, and cook for about 3 minutes. Season with salt and pepper to taste. Set aside.

Preheat the broiler.

In a small bowl, combine the butter and truffle oil. Rub the bread with the garlic halves. Brush the bread with the butter mixture. Season with salt and pepper to taste. Place the bread on a baking sheet and broil for about 5 minutes, or until browned.

Transfer the toasts to a cutting board and spoon the mushrooms on top. Cut into bite-sized pieces and arrange on a serving platter.

SERVES 6 TO 8

BREAD SUGGESTIONS
Crusty country, brioche, herb, olive, wheat, whole grain.

Nasturtium–Goat Cheese Toast with Raspberry-Beet Salad

5 MEDIUM BEETS

1 CINNAMON STICK

5 WHOLE CLOVES

1 SMALL ONION, THINLY SLICED

12 NASTURTIUM BLOSSOMS

6 OUNCES GOAT CHEESE (CHÈVRE) AT ROOM
TEMPERATURE

1/4 TEASPOON FRESHLY GROUND PEPPER,
PLUS MORE AS NEEDED

2 TABLESPOONS CHOPPED FRESH CHIVES

1 CUP RASPBERRIES

2 TABLESPOONS OLIVE OIL

1/2 CUP SEASONED RICE WINE VINEGAR

SALT

4 BREAD SLICES (EACH 1/2 INCH THICK)

This is a salad on top of toast. The combination of goat cheese and beets is unbeatable. Nasturtiums add color and a peppery quality. You can substitute other edible flowers such as roses, calendula, or chive or onion blossoms. Be sure to use organic ones.

Cut the greens and long roots off the beets. Reserve the greens if fresh and tender.

Wash the beets thoroughly and put in medium saucepan along with the cinnamon, cloves, and onion. Add water to cover the beets. Set over medium heat and simmer for about 30 minutes, or until the beets are tender when pierced with a knife. Drain the beets. When they are cool enough to handle, hold them under running water and, using your hands, slip off the skins. Cut the beets into bite-sized wedges and transfer to a small bowl.

Remove and chop the petals from 8 nasturtium blossoms. Put them in a small bowl and add the goat cheese, the 1/4 teaspoon pepper, and 1 tablespoon of the chives. Stir to blend. Let stand at room temperature.

In a medium bowl, using a fork, mash the raspberries. Add the remaining 1 tablespoon chives, the olive oil, and vinegar. Chop the reserved beet greens, if using, and add them along with the beets to the raspberry mixture. Season generously with salt and pepper to taste. Mound the beets and greens in the center of a serving platter.

Toast the bread and cut into wedges. Spread the goat cheese on the toasts and arrange them around the beets. Garnish with the remaining 4 nasturtium blossoms. Encourage diners to spoon the beets on top of the toasts.

SERVES 6

BREAD SUGGESTIONS
White, Italian, sourdough,
wheat, whole grain, brioche.

Toast with Smooshed Cauliflower and Bagna Cauda

I often remember opening my Italian grandmother's kitchen door to the aromas of garlic and anchovy. Bagna cauda, a warm dip made from anchovy and garlic, was a frequent offering at Nana's house. She used to serve her bagna cauda in a hot cast-iron skillet surrounded by crusty toasted bread and steamed cauliflower. I still like it that way but, in this recipe, I added the cauliflower to the bagna cauda ingredients, creating a perfect spread for crusty toast.

In a small bowl, combine the olive oil and garlic. Let stand for at least 15 minutes.

In a medium skillet over medium heat, warm 3 tablespoons of the garlic-infused olive oil along with about half of the garlic. Add the cauliflower and broth. Simmer, stirring occasionally, for about 15 minutes, or until the cauliflower can be easily smashed with a fork. Continue simmering and smashing the cauliflower, adding more broth if necessary, until the cauliflower is very soft, 5 to 7 minutes.

Transfer the cauliflower to a medium bowl. Add the anchovies, 1 1/2 tablespoons of the chives, and the red pepper flakes, if using. Season with black pepper to taste and stir to mix.

Preheat the broiler.

Brush the bread with the remaining olive oil and garlic. Place the bread on a baking sheet and broil for 3 to 4 minutes, or until the bread is lightly browned. Cut each slice into 2 or 4 pieces. Spoon some of the cauliflower mixture onto the toasts and arrange on a serving platter. Or, for a more rustic presentation, mound the cauliflower in the center of a platter and drizzle more olive oil over the top. Tear the toasts into pieces and arrange them around the cauliflower. Garnish with the remaining chopped chives.

SERVES 4

1/4 CUP EXTRA-VIRGIN OLIVE OIL

3 CLOVES GARLIC, MINCED

1 SMALL HEAD CAULIFLOWER, CORED AND CUT INTO SMALL FLORETS

2 CUPS CHICKEN OR VEGETABLE BROTH, PLUS MORE AS NEEDED

5 OR 6 ANCHOVY FILLETS, CHOPPED

2 TABLESPOONS CHOPPED FRESH CHIVES

1/4 TEASPOON RED PEPPER FLAKES (OPTIONAL)

FRESHLY GROUND BLACK PEPPER

6 BREAD SLICES

BREAD SUGGESTIONS
Italian, white, wheat, baguette, hard rolls, chapatti, foccacia

Toast with Chopped Chicken Liver

OK, this is a confession. Some people cannot keep ice cream or candy around the house because they will eat it all. Me? I am like that with really good chopped chicken liver, the kind my mom makes. I can eat chopped liver on toast (or matzos) for breakfast, lunch, dinner, or a midnight snack.

4 TABLESPOONS UNSALTED BUTTER OR CHICKEN FAT

1 POUND YELLOW ONIONS, SLICED

1 POUND CHICKEN LIVERS, WASHED AND ANY MEMBRANES REMOVED

2 TABLESPOONS BRANDY

4 HARD-BOILED EGGS, GRATED, PLUS MORE FOR GARNISHING

SALT AND FRESHLY GROUND PEPPER

6 TO 8 BREAD SLICES

CHOPPED FRESH FLAT-LEAF PARSLEY FOR GARNISHING

In a medium skillet over medium heat, melt the butter. Add the onions and cook, stirring occasionally, for about 15 minutes, or until soft and golden brown. Using a slotted spoon, transfer the onions to a food processor, reserving the butter and juices in the skillet.

In the same skillet, add the chicken livers and sauté for about 10 minutes, or until they are cooked through but still slightly pink in the middle. Add the brandy and cook for 1 minute longer. Transfer the livers and juices to the food processor. Chop the onions and chicken livers to the desired consistency, either coarse or smooth. Add the 4 grated eggs and chop for 15 seconds longer. Season with salt and pepper to taste.

Toast the bread and cut into bite-sized pieces. Mound the chopped liver in the center of a serving platter and surround with the toasts. Garnish with grated eggs and parsley.

SERVES 6 TO 8

MAKE-AHEAD TIP
Chopped liver, like soup, tastes even better the next day. It keeps for about 3 days refrigerated.

BREAD SUGGESTIONS
Rye, white, baguette, wheat, challah.

Toast with Tomatoes, Anchovies, and Capers

2 LARGE TOMATOES (ABOUT 1 POUND),
SEEDED AND COARSELY CHOPPED

2 TEASPOONS CHOPPED FRESH ROSEMARY

1 TABLESPOON CAPERS

5 ANCHOVIES, CHOPPED

1 CLOVE GARLIC, MINCED

3 TABLESPOONS EXTRA-VIRGIN OLIVE OIL

1 1/2 TABLESPOONS BALSAMIC VINEGAR

SALT AND FRESHLY GROUND PEPPER

SUGAR, IF NEEDED

12 SMALL BREAD SLICES

This classic toast, known in Italy as bruschetta, tastes best when made with the very best sun-ripened tomatoes. But when fresh tomatoes are out of season, substitute sun-dried ones. If you use tomatoes preserved in olive oil, omit the olive oil called for in this recipe. Here, as with any dish that includes tomatoes, a touch of sugar can help boost the flavor.

In a medium bowl, combine the tomatoes, rosemary, capers, anchovies, garlic, olive oil, and vinegar. Season with salt and pepper to taste. Taste and add sugar if needed. Let stand at room temperature for at least 15 minutes.

Toast the bread. Mound the tomato mixture on the toasts and arrange on a platter.

SERVES 6 TO 8

MAKE-AHEAD TIP
Prepare the tomato mixture ahead of time and refrigerate. Bring to room temperature before serving.

BREAD SUGGESTIONS
Italian, baguette, pugliese, any crusty, hearty bread.

Little Toasts with Smoked Whitefish and Apples

The pairing of salty whitefish and crisp, sweet apples is a natural for Champagne. I like to use thick slices of bread for the toast. It makes this appetizer more rustic in style. You can substitute dry smoked salmon or any other smoked fish for the whitefish.

In a small bowl, combine the sour cream, onion, whitefish, apple, and basil.

Toast the bread and cut into wedges. Mound the whitefish mixture in the center of a serving platter and surround with the toasts. Or, spread the mixture on the toasts and arrange on a platter. Garnish with chives.

SERVES 4 TO 6

1 CUP SOUR CREAM

2 TABLESPOONS FINELY CHOPPED RED ONION

1 CUP CRUMBLED SMOKED WHITEFISH

1/2 CUP FINELY CHOPPED APPLE

2 TABLESPOONS CHOPPED FRESH BASIL

4 BREAD SLICES (EACH 1/2 INCH THICK)

CHOPPED FRESH CHIVES FOR GARNISHING

BREAD SUGGESTIONS
White, sourdough, rye, brioche.

Little Toasts with Shrimp Pâté and Cucumbers

6 OUNCES COOKED SHRIMP, FINELY CHOPPED

6 OUNCES CREAM CHEESE AT ROOM
TEMPERATURE

1 GREEN ONION (BOTH WHITE AND GREEN
PARTS), FINELY CHOPPED

2 TABLESPOONS CHOPPED FRESH DILL

2 TABLESPOONS SWEET VERMOUTH

SALT AND FRESHLY GROUND PEPPER

1/4 CUCUMBER, PEELED, SEEDED, AND
FINELY CHOPPED

1 TABLESPOON SEASONED RICE WINE VINEGAR

6 BREAD SLICES, QUARTERED

We do a lot of catering, especially at Stanford University's Cantor Arts Center, where we operate the museum café. This appetizer is one of the most popular. In fact, we served it when we catered a party for Chelsea Clinton's graduation from Stanford in the spring of 2001. This recipe makes slightly less than what we prepared for the Clinton event!

Preheat a broiler or use a toaster oven.

In a medium bowl, combine the shrimp, cream cheese, green onion, 1 1/2 tablespoons of the dill, and the vermouth. Stir to blend thoroughly. Season with salt and pepper to taste.

In a small bowl, combine the cucumber and vinegar. Season with a pinch of salt.

Place the bread on a baking sheet and broil for 3 to 4 minutes, or toast in a toaster oven. Put the shrimp pâté in the center of a serving platter, using your hands to form a mound. Top with the cucumber and surround with the toasts. Or, spread the pâté on the toasts, top each with a pinch of the cucumber, and arrange on a platter.

Garnish with the remaining 1/2 tablespoon dill.

SERVES 6 TO 8

BREAD SUGGESTIONS
White, sourdough, Italian, brioche.

Toast with Smoked Chicken, Strawberries, and Chives

4 BREAD SLICES

6 TABLESPOONS CREAM CHEESE AT ROOM
TEMPERATURE

1 TABLESPOON SUGAR

1 SMOKED CHICKEN BREAST (ABOUT 6 OUNCES)

4 TO 6 VERY SWEET STRAWBERRIES, SLICED

1 TABLESPOON CHOPPED FRESH CHIVES

Strawberries are not just for dessert—they also complement smoky foods beautifully. Try to use organic strawberries in this dish. When not organically grown, strawberries can be heavily sprayed with pesticides. For health and environmental reasons, I encourage using organically grown fruits and vegetables wherever they are available, but it is especially important with strawberries. If you can't find smoked chicken, substitute smoked turkey, ham, or even smoked Cheddar cheese.

Toast the bread.

In a small bowl, combine the cream cheese and sugar. Spread the cream cheese mixture on the toasts.

Remove the skin from the chicken breast and thinly slice the meat. Arrange the slices on top of the cream cheese. Cut the toast into bite-sized pieces. Top with the strawberries and sprinkle with the chives. Arrange on a serving platter.

SERVES 4 TO 6

BREAD SUGGESTIONS
Wheat, white, raisin, brioche, bagels, English muffins, crumpets.

Little Meatballs on Garlic Toast

Toast

12 BREAD SLICES

3 TABLESPOONS EXTRA-VIRGIN OLIVE OIL

1 CLOVE GARLIC, HALVED

Meatballs

1/4 CUP MILK

1 EGG

2 TABLESPOONS KETCHUP

1 1/2 POUNDS GROUND MEAT

2 CLOVES GARLIC, MINCED

3 TABLESPOONS GRATED YELLOW ONION

1 TEASPOON SALT

1/4 TEASPOON FRESHLY GROUND PEPPER

2 TEASPOONS DRIED ITALIAN SEASONING

1/2 CUP CHOPPED FRESH FLAT-LEAF PARSLEY

At parties, this homey little appetizer can be the most popular in the midst of fancier, more impressive offerings. I am always amazed at how fast they disappear. The meatballs can be made from any kind of ground meat. Besides beef, consider turkey, chicken, pork, or lamb.

TO MAKE THE TOAST: Preheat the broiler. Using a 2-inch round cookie cutter, cut out 20 rounds of bread. Reserve the leftover bread from 3 slices for the meatballs. Place the bread rounds on a baking sheet. Brush the rounds with the olive oil and then rub with the garlic. Broil for about 3 minutes, or until lightly browned. Set aside.

Turn off the broiler. Preheat the oven to 400 degrees F. Lightly oil a baking sheet.

TO MAKE THE MEATBALLS: Put the reserved leftover bread in a medium bowl. Add the milk and egg and, using your hands, mix it all together. Add the ketchup, ground meat, garlic, onion, salt, pepper, Italian seasoning, and 1/4 cup of the parsley. Mix thoroughly. Form the meat mixture into 20 meatballs and place them on the prepared baking sheet. Bake for 12 to 15 minutes, or until browned and cooked through in the center.

Cut the meatballs in half and arrange 2 halves, cut-side down, slightly overlapping, on each round of toast. Garnish with the remaining parsley and arrange on a serving platter.

SERVES 6 TO 10

MAKE-AHEAD TIP

Meatballs freeze well. Bake them and freeze individually, then store in a sealable plastic bag. Reheat the frozen meatballs in a microwave for 1 minute, or warm them in a toaster oven.

BREAD SUGGESTIONS

White, wheat, sourdough, potato, whole grain.

Garlic Bread Cooked over an Open Fire

6 TABLESPOONS BUTTER (IF USING SALTED BUTTER, OMIT THE SALT IN THE RECIPE)

1 TEASPOON SALT

3 TABLESPOONS EXTRA-VIRGIN OLIVE OIL

6 CLOVES GARLIC, MINCED

1 TEASPOON SWEET PAPRIKA

¹/₈ CUP CHOPPED FRESH CHIVES

1 LOAF FLAT ITALIAN BREAD

BREAD SUGGESTIONS
Italian, sourdough, ciabatta, focaccia, herb, olive, wheat.

If you have ever gone camping, you know that anything cooked over an open fire tastes fabulous. And so it is with toast. There is an art to making toast over the fire. Unless you are like my mother and love burned toast, you need to toast bread over medium-hot coals and not over the flame itself. When the heat or flame is too hot, the bread will cook too quickly. For this garlic toast, I wrap it in foil, so the garlic and butter won't drip off the bread, sparking the coals. Even through the foil, the garlic bread takes on a delicious smoky flavor from the burning embers. This bread makes a wonderful accompaniment to just about anything cooked outdoors (or indoors, for that matter). If you are backpacking or camping without refrigeration, use only olive oil, increasing it to replace the butter. Use garlic powder instead of fresh garlic, and combine it with the oil, salt, paprika, and chives in a well-sealed jar or plastic container. Take along a brush, or drizzle the olive oil on the bread just before grilling.

In a medium bowl, combine the butter, salt, olive oil, garlic, paprika, and chives. Cut the bread in half horizontally. Spread the butter mixture evenly on both cut sides. Wrap each half with aluminum foil, sealing it tightly and forming a seam on the unbuttered side. If you want more of a smoky flavor, don't wrap the bread in foil.

For foil-wrapped bread, put it far enough away from the fire to warm it thoroughly yet close enough to absorb the smoky flavors. Cook for about 15 minutes, opening the foil occasionally to check if the butter has completely melted. For unwrapped bread, put the halves, buttered-side up, directly on the grill. Turn them over and brown slightly, but don't let too much of the butter melt into the fire.

Remove from the heat and cut into slices.

SERVES 4 TO 6

Sandwiches

I could have written an entire book about toasted sandwiches because

I love them so much. At one of my restaurants, jZcool Eatery and Catering Company in Menlo Park, California, we toast most of our sandwiches. We use several methods for toasting the bread—panini grills, a broiler, a well-seasoned flat-top griddle, and an open-flame grill. But these commercial methods are no different from using your own home appliances, such as an upright toaster, a toaster oven, a heavy-bottomed skillet, a broiler, or an outdoor grill.

As for the type of bread, don't limit yourself to wheat, white, or sourdough. Try focaccia, baguette, or even hard rolls for wonderful, extra-toasty sandwiches. And experiment with the fillings. Tuck ham and cheese, or wilted spinach and ricotta, or turkey and caramelized onions between the bread slices and brush the outside with a little butter or oil. Then toast the sandwich until the outside is browned and crisp, while the inside is soft and sensual, bursting with flavor.

Toasted sandwiches can also be open-faced: toast the bread, then pile on the luscious ingredients and toast it again under the broiler until everything is bubbly and browned.

The sandwiches in this chapter can also be transformed into appetizers by cutting them into bite-sized pieces. Egg and Fennel Salad on Toast with Caviar (page 55) would make an impressive hors d'oeuvre for a special occasion.

Many of these recipes are from jZcool, where I get great pleasure when I see a customer, sitting at one of our butcher-block tables, sandwich in hand, nearly speechless because the sandwich is that outrageous.

Egg and Fennel Salad on Toast with Caviar

I love sipping a glass of crisp French-style rosé with this toast. It is a rustic yet elegant dish that takes egg salad to new heights. The recipe calls for 2 to 3 ounces of caviar, but the amount you use depends on your taste and budget. If desired, cut the toasts into quarters and serve the egg salad as canapés, topped with caviar.

1 SMALL FENNEL BULB (ABOUT 4 OUNCES)

2 TABLESPOONS CHOPPED RED ONION

1 1/2 TEASPOONS DIJON MUSTARD

1 TEASPOON SUGAR

1/4 TEASPOON SWEET PAPRIKA

2 TABLESPOONS CHOPPED FRESH FLAT-LEAF PARSLEY

8 HARD-BOILED EGGS, COARSELY GRATED

1/2 CUP MAYONNAISE, OR AS NEEDED

SALT AND FRESHLY GROUND PEPPER

4 BREAD SLICES

2 TO 3 OUNCES CAVIAR OF YOUR CHOICE

Trim away the green fronds and the base of the fennel. Remove and discard the outer leaves. Finely chop the inner bulb.

In a medium bowl, combine the fennel, onion, mustard, sugar, paprika, parsley, and eggs. Add enough mayonnaise to make a soft pâté-like mixture. Season lightly with salt and pepper to taste (remember that caviar is salty).

Toast the bread. Mound the egg salad in the center of the toasts, to within 1 inch of the edges. Top each with a dollop of caviar.

SERVES 4

BREAD SUGGESTIONS
Brioche, white, wheat, rye, challah.

Toasted Sandwiches with Leeks, Goat Cheese, and Thyme

4 TABLESPOONS UNSALTED BUTTER

6 LARGE LEEKS (TOUGH GREEN LEAVES REMOVED), SLICED AND THOROUGHLY WASHED

1 TABLESPOON CHOPPED FRESH THYME

1/2 TEASPOON RED PEPPER FLAKES, OR AS NEEDED (OPTIONAL)

4 BREAD SLICES

4 OUNCES GOAT CHEESE (CHÈVRE) AT ROOM TEMPERATURE

SALT AND FRESHLY GROUND BLACK PEPPER

1 1/2 TABLESPOONS STONE-GROUND MUSTARD

I am enticed by any dish with slow-cooked leeks. In this sandwich, sweet, buttery leeks are paired with creamy goat cheese to create a rich, luscious sandwich—it's one you'll think of when you hunger for a special treat. These sandwiches would also make a great appetizer. Cut each one into 4 triangles. Set a small bowl of mango chutney in the middle of a platter and surround with the sandwiches.

In a large sauté pan over medium-low heat, warm 2 tablespoons of the butter. Add the leeks and cook, stirring occasionally, for about 15 minutes, until they are very soft. Add the thyme and red pepper flakes, if using. Set aside.

Lightly spread the remaining 2 tablespoons butter on the bread. Place 2 of the slices, buttered-side down, in a large skillet. Top with the leeks and crumble the goat cheese on top. Season lightly with salt and black pepper to taste.

Lightly spread the mustard on the unbuttered side of the remaining 2 bread slices. Cover each sandwich with 1 bread slice, buttered-side up.

Set the skillet over medium heat. Cover and cook the sandwiches, turning once, for 3 to 4 minutes per side, or until browned. Remove the sandwiches from the skillet, let stand for a few minutes, and cut in half.

SERVES 2

BREAD SUGGESTIONS
Whole grain, sourdough, white, rye, herb.

My Mom's Ooey-Gooey Cheese Sandwiches with Tomato-Pear Chutney

1 CAN (16 OUNCES) CHOPPED TOMATOES

2 CUPS PEELED AND CHOPPED PEARS
(ABOUT 1 POUND)

1 MEDIUM ONION, COARSELY CHOPPED

1 CUP RAISINS

2 CUPS FIRMLY PACKED LIGHT BROWN SUGAR

1 CUP CIDER VINEGAR

1/4 CUP PEELED CHOPPED FRESH GINGER

2 TABLESPOONS MUSTARD SEED

2 CINNAMON STICKS

2 SPICY CHILES, SEEDED AND CHOPPED

2 TEASPOONS SALT

4 HARD ROLLS

8 OUNCES GOAT CHEESE (CHÈVRE)

6 OUNCES JACK CHEESE, SLICED

3 TABLESPOONS GRATED ASIAGO CHEESE

1/8 CUP CHOPPED FRESH FLAT-LEAF PARSLEY

Most professional cooks have their favorite sauces or homemade condiments, affectionately referred to as "mother sauces." They are used over and over in a variety of ways because they are so versatile. I have my favorites, too, and they have become the backbone to the success and continuity of my cooking. Tomato-pear chutney tops my list. This luscious sandwich was inspired by and is certainly dedicated to my mom, the lovely June Ziff. This recipe makes 6 pints and keeps for 1 month refrigerated. If you don't have time to make chutney, there are many delicious prepared ones available in specialty grocery stores.

TO MAKE THE CHUTNEY: In a medium saucepan, combine the tomatoes, pears, onion, raisins, brown sugar, vinegar, ginger, mustard seed, cinnamon sticks, chiles, and salt. Set the pan over medium heat and simmer, stirring occasionally, for 1 hour, or until the fruit is soft and the chutney begins to thicken. Remove the cinnamon stick and set aside.

Preheat the broiler. Cut the rolls in half horizontally and place them, cut-sides up, on a baking sheet. Spoon a generous amount of chutney onto the bottom halves of the rolls. Crumble the goat cheese on top. Put the Jack cheese and sprinkle the Asiago cheese on the top halves of the rolls. Broil for about 5 minutes, or until the cheese melts and the bread is toasty brown. Remove from the broiler and sprinkle with the parsley. Place the top halves on the bottom halves. Let the sandwiches stand for a few minutes and cut in half.

SERVES 2

BREAD SUGGESTIONS
Crusty rolls, baguette,
English muffins.

Roasted Chicken Sandwiches with Spinach and Red Bell Peppers

1 BUNCH SPINACH, STEMMED, WASHED, AND COARSELY CHOPPED

1 TABLESPOON EXTRA-VIRGIN OLIVE OIL

1 CLOVE GARLIC, MINCED

1 TO 2 TABLESPOONS BALSAMIC VINEGAR

1 1/2 TABLESPOONS MAYONNAISE

2 TEASPOONS DIJON MUSTARD

1/2 TEASPOON HONEY

4 BREAD SLICES

2 VERY THIN ROUNDS RED ONION

4 VERY THIN SLICES RED BELL PEPPER

SALT AND FRESHLY GROUND PEPPER

6 TO 8 OUNCES COOKED CHICKEN, SLICED

These days, you can easily find rotisserie chicken in most neighborhood grocery stores. This recipe is also a great way to use up leftover roasted chicken from the previous night's dinner. If you'd like, substitute oven-roasted ripe tomatoes for the bell peppers.

In a steamer basket over a pot of boiling water, cook the spinach for about 5 minutes, or until very wilted. Transfer the spinach to a colander and let cool. Using your hands or a towel, squeeze out most of the liquid. Put the spinach in a small bowl, add the olive oil, garlic, and vinegar and stir to mix.

In another small bowl, combine the mayonnaise, mustard, and honey.

Toast the bread. Spread the mayonnaise mixture on 2 slices of toast. Top each with 1 onion round and 2 bell pepper slices. Season with salt and pepper to taste. Evenly distribute the chicken on top of the peppers and top with the spinach. Drizzle any juices from the spinach over the remaining 2 slices of plain toast.

Cover each sandwich with a slice of plain toast and press down firmly. Cut the sandwiches in half.

SERVES 2

BREAD SUGGESTIONS
Whole grain, white, sourdough, olive, herb, rye, focaccia, pugliese.

Tarragon-Crusted Salmon with Olive-Caper Aioli on Toast

1 EGG YOLK

1 TABLESPOON SEASONED RICE WINE VINEGAR

2 CLOVES GARLIC, MINCED

3/4 CUP EXTRA-VIRGIN OLIVE OIL, PLUS MORE
FOR RUBBING SALMON

1/4 CUP PITTED KALAMATA OLIVES, FINELY
CHOPPED

1 ROUNDED TABLESPOON CAPERS

2 TEASPOONS LEMON ZEST

SALT AND FRESHLY GROUND PEPPER

1 SALMON FILLET (ABOUT 12 OUNCES)

JUICE OF 1 LEMON

3 TABLESPOONS FRESH TARRAGON, OR
1 TEASPOON DRIED

4 BREAD SLICES

2 TABLESPOONS CHOPPED FRESH CHIVES

Make big open-faced sandwiches or serve the salmon in the middle of a platter, surrounded with toast points spread with the olive-caper aioli.

In a food processor or using a whisk and bowl, process or whisk the egg yolk with the vinegar and garlic. Slowly add the 3/4 cup olive oil, processing or whisking continuously until the aioli thickens. Fold in the olives, capers, and lemon zest. Season with salt and pepper to taste. Cover and refrigerate until ready to use.

Preheat the broiler.

Rub the salmon with olive oil and place on a small baking sheet. Sprinkle the lemon juice and tarragon over the salmon. Season with salt and pepper to taste. Broil for about 6 minutes, or until done to your liking. Let cool to room temperature.

Toast the bread. Generously spread the aioli on the toasts. Break the salmon into pieces and arrange it evenly on top. Garnish with the chives.

SERVES 4

MAKE-AHEAD TIP
Roast the salmon, cover, and refrigerate. The olive-aioli mixture can be prepared up to two weeks ahead and refrigerated. Serve the fish chilled or at room temperature.

BREAD SUGGESTIONS
Sourdough, whole grain, white, baguette, rye, brioche, pugliese.

Prawns, Avocado, and Feta on Toast

1/2 POUND PEELED COOKED PRAWNS, CUT INTO
BITE-SIZED PIECES

1 MEDIUM RIPE TOMATO, SEEDED AND CUT INTO
BITE-SIZED PIECES

1/4 CUP FINELY CHOPPED RED ONION

1/4 CUP CHOPPED FRESH CILANTRO

1 JALAPEÑO CHILE, SEEDED AND FINELY
CHOPPED

3/4 TEASPOON GROUND CUMIN

JUICE OF 1 LIME

1 AVOCADO, PITTED, PEELED, AND CUT INTO
BITE-SIZED PIECES

SALT AND FRESHLY GROUND PEPPER

1 BAGUETTE

3 TABLESPOONS OLIVE OIL

2 CLOVES GARLIC, HALVED

4 OUNCES FETA, CRUMBLED

This festive open-faced sandwich would also make a wonderful brunch offering. Serve it alongside fried eggs, or scramble the ingredients with eggs and accompany with toast.

In a medium bowl, combine the prawns, tomato, onion, cilantro, chile, cumin, lime juice, and avocado. Season with salt and pepper to taste and stir to mix. Cover and refrigerate until ready to use.

Preheat the broiler.

Cut the baguette into 4 pieces, then cut each piece in half horizontally. Place the baguette halves, cut-sides up, on a baking sheet. Using your hands, scoop out about one-third of the bread from inside each half, creating a long cavity. Brush the cavities with olive oil and then rub with the garlic. Sprinkle the feta in each cavity. Broil for about 4 minutes, or until the bread is browned and the cheese is melted.

Spoon the prawn mixture into the baguette cavities and serve.

SERVES 4

BREAD SUGGESTIONS
Baguette, hard rolls.

Toasted Sandwiches with Ham, Brie, Capers, and Honey Mustard

4 TABLESPOONS STONE-GROUND MUSTARD

1 TEASPOON HONEY

$1/2$ TEASPOON DRIED THYME

8 BREAD SLICES

12 OUNCES HAM, SLICED

4 VERY THIN ROUNDS RED ONION

6 OUNCES BRIE OR CAMEMBERT CHEESE, CUT INTO SMALL PIECES

2 TEASPOONS CAPERS

3 TABLESPOONS UNSALTED BUTTER

I love this combination of ham with honey mustard and capers. The Brie adds a touch of richness. You can buy store-bought sweetened mustards, but it is so easy to make your own, as you'll discover in this recipe. If you can find green or black olive bread, I think it is the best choice for these sandwiches. For an extraordinary open-faced version, divide the ingredients among all of the bread slices and broil for about 6 minutes.

In a small bowl, combine the mustard, honey, and thyme. Spread a thin layer on the bread and top 4 of the bread slices with the ham. Pull the onion rings apart and arrange them on top of the ham. Scatter the cheese on the onions, and sprinkle the capers on top. Cover each sandwich with 1 bread slice, mustard-side down, and press down to secure the capers.

In a large, heavy skillet over medium-low heat, melt $1^1/2$ tablespoons of the butter. Place the sandwiches in the skillet and reduce the heat to low. Cover and cook the sandwiches for about 4 minutes, or until browned on one side. Uncover and add the remaining $1^1/2$ tablespoons butter to the outside edges of the pan to melt it. Turn the sandwiches over, spreading the melted butter. Cover and cook for about 4 minutes, or until browned on the other side.

Remove the sandwiches from the skillet and let stand for a few minutes before serving.

SERVES 4

BREAD SUGGESTIONS
Olive, sour dough, white, brioche, rosemary, cheese.

Toasted Sandwiches with Turkey, Provolone, and Caramelized Onions

I could eat this sandwich several times a week. I like caramelized onions so much, I can never put too many on the sandwich. The sweetness of the onions complements the turkey and provolone cheese beautifully. Accompany the sandwiches with little bowls of sweet pickles, spicy chutneys, and hot sauces.

In a medium skillet over medium-low heat, warm the olive oil. Add the onion and cook, stirring occasionally, for about 20 minutes, or until golden brown and very soft. Transfer the onion to a bowl, but do not clean the skillet.

Spread a generous amount of the onion on 2 of the bread slices. Top with the turkey and cheese. Lightly spread the mustard on the remaining 2 bread slices. Cover each sandwich with 1 bread slice, mustard-side down.

Place the sandwiches in the same skillet you used to cook the onion and set over medium heat. Cook the sandwiches, turning once, for about 4 minutes per side, or until the sandwiches are browned on both sides and the cheese is melted. Remove the sandwiches from the skillet, let stand for a few minutes, and cut in half or into quarters.

SERVES 2

1 TABLESPOON OLIVE OIL

1 LARGE YELLOW ONION, THINLY SLICED

4 HAND-CUT BREAD SLICES (EACH 3/4 INCH THICK)

6 OUNCES TURKEY BREAST, SLICED

3 OUNCES PROVOLONE CHEESE, SLICED

2 TABLESPOONS DIJON MUSTARD

BREAD SUGGESTIONS
Sourdough, rye, whole grain, focaccia, herb.

Eggplant, Red Bell Peppers, Mozzarella, and Arugula Sandwiches

SALT

1/2 GLOBE EGGPLANT, CUT INTO 1-INCH PIECES

1 MEDIUM RED BELL PEPPER, SEEDED, DERIBBED, AND CUT INTO 1/2-INCH PIECES

3 LARGE GARLIC BULBS, HALVED HORIZONTALLY

4 TABLESPOONS EXTRA-VIRGIN OLIVE OIL

2 CLOVES GARLIC, MINCED

3 TABLESPOONS CHOPPED FRESH OREGANO

1 BAGUETTE

8 OUNCES FRESH MOZZARELLA CHEESE, SLICED

3 TABLESPOONS BALSAMIC VINEGAR

1 SMALL BUNCH ARUGULA, STEMMED

FRESHLY GROUND PEPPER

Eggplant, bell peppers, and fresh mozzarella give these toasts a Mediterranean feel. Arugula adds a California twist.

Preheat the oven to 375 degrees F.

Lightly salt the eggplant and drain in a colander for 15 minutes.

In a medium bowl, combine the eggplant, bell pepper, and garlic bulbs. Toss with 1 tablespoon of the olive oil, the minced garlic, and oregano. Place on a baking sheet and roast, stirring occasionally, for about 45 minutes, or until the vegetables are soft. Set aside to cool, but do not turn off the oven.

When the garlic is cool enough to handle, squeeze the soft cloves into a small bowl.

Cut the baguette in half horizontally. Place the halves, cut-sides up, on a baking sheet. Spread the roasted garlic on one half. Place the mozzarella on the other half. Bake for about 10 minutes, or until lightly browned.

Meanwhile, in a medium bowl, combine the remaining 3 tablespoons olive oil, the vinegar, and arugula. Season with salt and pepper to taste.

Remove the baguette from the oven. Spread the eggplant and bell pepper on the half with the roasted garlic. Top with the arugula salad and cover with the other half of the baguette. Press down with your hands and cut into slices.

SERVES 4 TO 6

MAKE-AHEAD TIP

Roast the eggplant, bell peppers, and garlic up to 1 day ahead. Rewarm the vegetables, then assemble and bake the sandwich as directed.

BREAD SUGGESTIONS

Baguette, hard rolls, focaccia, ciabatta.

Main Courses

I rarely sit down to a meal without a basket of bread nearby. I love the crust and use it, along with my fork, to gather up every last bite and juicy morsel.

Toast for dinner can be as classic as Welsh Rarebit and Tomatoes (page 70). Or hold the buns and use thick slices of toast for scrumptious turkey burgers (page 74). I never tire of the Italian-style bread salad known as Panzanella (page 79). Here, I toss bite-sized pieces of toast with tomatoes, chicken, and fresh basil. In Pot Roast on Toast (page 76), the meat and juices are piled heartily on top of toast. Supper couldn't be homier than this.

I love steamers, so a bowl of garlicky mussels resting on top of toast that is drenched in a broth of olive oil, wine, and Pernod (page 72) is beyond compare. I hope some of these recipes will inspire you to enjoy toast for dinner in ways you might otherwise never have considered.

Tuna Melts with Avocado and Emmentaler Cheese

1 FRESH TUNA FILLET (ABOUT 8 OUNCES)

1 TABLESPOON EXTRA-VIRGIN OLIVE OIL

2 LEMON SLICES

SALT AND FRESHLY GROUND PEPPER

1 SMALL FENNEL BULB (ABOUT 4 OUNCES)

1/4 CUP CHOPPED RED ONION

1 TEASPOON DIJON MUSTARD

1/2 CUP MAYONNAISE

3 TABLESPOONS SWEET PICKLE RELISH

DASH OF HOT SAUCE

4 BREAD SLICES (EACH 3/4 INCH THICK)

1 AVOCADO, PITTED, PEELED, AND SLICED

6 OUNCES EMMENTALER CHEESE, GRATED

Using fresh or fresh-frozen tuna instead of canned makes this down-home sandwich extraordinary. If tuna is unavailable, ask for a similar firm, flaky fish, such as halibut, swordfish, or even salmon. Whenever you are having fish for dinner, cook an extra piece, refrigerate overnight, and use it in these sandwiches. Accompany with a full-flavored ale or stout.

In a small sauté pan over medium heat, combine the tuna, olive oil, lemon, and about 1/2 cup water. Season with salt and pepper to taste. Cover and cook for about 6 minutes, or until the fish flakes easily with a fork. Transfer to a bowl, cover, and refrigerate for at least 2 hours.

Trim away the green fronds and the base of the fennel. Remove and discard the outer leaves. Finely chop the inner bulb.

In a medium bowl, combine the fennel, onion, mustard, mayonnaise, and relish. Break the tuna into small pieces and add to the bowl. Season with hot sauce and salt and pepper to taste.

Preheat the broiler. Place the bread on a baking sheet and broil for about 3 to 4 minutes, or until lightly toasted.

Mound the tuna salad on the toasts. Top with the avocado and cheese, pressing lightly on the cheese. Broil for 4 to 5 minutes, or until the cheese is bubbly.

SERVES 4

BREAD SUGGESTIONS
Sourdough, white, Italian, whole grain, rye, wheat.

Toast with Welsh Rarebit and Tomatoes

1 POUND CHEDDAR CHEESE, GRATED

1 TEASPOON SWEET PAPRIKA

1/4 TEASPOON CAYENNE PEPPER

1 TEASPOON DRY MUSTARD

2 TABLESPOONS UNSALTED BUTTER

1 CUP ALE

SALT AND FRESHLY GROUND BLACK PEPPER

4 BREAD SLICES

8 TOMATO SLICES (EACH ABOUT 1/2 INCH THICK)

CHOPPED FRESH CHIVES FOR GARNISHING

This recipe comes from a very old cookbook I found in a used bookstore. Entitled *The Modern Cook Book and Household Recipes*, it was written in 1904 and is a collection of traditional recipes used by home cooks at the turn of the twentieth century. The tomato helps cut the richness of the rarebit. Rarebit is wonderful with the addition of fresh crab. Mound a generous handful of crabmeat on top of the tomatoes before pouring on the rarebit sauce. Serve with bottles of ice-cold ale or hearty beer.

In a saucepan over medium heat, melt the cheese, stirring occasionally. Add the paprika, cayenne, mustard, and 1 tablespoon of the butter. Gradually add the ale, stirring constantly. Season with salt and black pepper to taste. Keep warm.

Toast the bread. Spread the remaining 1 tablespoon butter on the toast.

Place 1 slice of toast in each of 4 shallow soup bowls. Top each with 2 tomato slices and season with salt and black pepper to taste. Pour the rarebit sauce over the toast and garnish with chives.

SERVES 4

BREAD SUGGESTIONS
Wheat, black, white, rye, sourdough, English muffins, crumpets.

Toast with Crab and Tarragon-Chive Sauce

1 POUND CRABMEAT, PICKED OVER FOR SHELLS

1/2 CUP CHOPPED RED BELL PEPPER

1 LARGE BUNCH FRESH CHIVES, CHOPPED

1/2 CUP MAYONNAISE, PLUS MORE AS NEEDED

1 TABLESPOON DIJON MUSTARD

1/4 TEASPOON HOT SAUCE

2 TEASPOONS LEMON ZEST

SALT AND FRESHLY GROUND PEPPER

6 TABLESPOONS UNSALTED BUTTER

1 CLOVE GARLIC, MINCED

2 TABLESPOONS CHOPPED FRESH TARRAGON

1/2 CUP DRY WHITE WINE

4 BREAD SLICES

2 TABLESPOONS CHOPPED FRESH FLAT-LEAF PARSLEY

The quality of the crab makes all the difference in this dish. Spend the extra money for fresh whole crabs or fresh-picked crabmeat. You can substitute cooked salmon or prawns for the crabmeat.

In a medium bowl, combine the crabmeat, bell pepper, chives, the 1/2 cup mayonnaise, the mustard, hot sauce, and lemon zest. Add more mayonnaise if you prefer. Season with salt and pepper to taste. Refrigerate until ready to use.

In a medium saucepan over medium heat, melt the butter with the garlic. Add the tarragon and gradually pour in the wine, whisking constantly. Reduce the heat to low and cook, whisking, for about 2 minutes, or until the sauce thickens slightly. Season with salt and pepper to taste. Keep warm until ready to serve.

Toast the bread. Place 1 slice of toast on each of 4 plates or on a large serving platter. Mound the crab mixture in the center of the toasts. Drizzle with the sauce, drizzling most of it on the toast. Garnish with the parsley.

SERVES 4

BREAD SUGGESTIONS
White, sourdough, Italian, olive, brioche, wheat.

Toast with Mussels, Fennel, and Pernod

1 SMALL FENNEL BULB (ABOUT 4 OUNCES)

1/4 CUP EXTRA-VIRGIN OLIVE OIL

2 LARGE SHALLOTS, CHOPPED

1 SMALL RED BELL PEPPER, CHOPPED

8 PEPPERCORNS

1 1/2 CUPS CLAM JUICE

6 CLOVES GARLIC, MINCED

1/2 CUP CHOPPED FRESH FLAT-LEAF PARSLEY

1/2 CUP DRY WHITE WINE (SUCH AS
CHARDONNAY, SAUVIGNON BLANC,
OR PINOT GRIGIO)

2 TO 3 TABLESPOONS PERNOD

SALT

2 POUNDS MUSSELS, SCRUBBED AND
DEBEARDED

4 BREAD SLICES (EACH 1/2 INCH THICK)

I enjoy this dish with abandon, often until my belly is full and the satisfaction is beyond words. I eat more mussels and toast than I care to admit. One piece of toast, placed under the mussels, is destined to become soggy. The others wait nearby, ready to be torn into crunchy pieces for soaking up the very last drops of the irresistible juices. If you'd like, add clams, prawns, or other shellfish along with the mussels.

Trim away the green fronds and the base of the fennel. Remove and discard the outer leaves. Thinly slice the inner bulb.

In a pot large enough to hold all of the mussels, warm the olive oil over medium heat. Add the fennel, shallots, and bell pepper and sauté, stirring occasionally, for 5 minutes. Add the peppercorns, clam juice, garlic, parsley, wine, and Pernod. Season generously with salt to taste. Add the mussels and stir them in the juices. Cover and steam for about 8 minutes, or until the mussels open. Discard any that do not open.

Toast the bread. Place 1 slice of toast in each of 2 large, shallow bowls. Spoon the mussels over the toasts and pour the juices over the mussels. Accompany with a plate of the extra toasts for dipping.

SERVES 2

BREAD SUGGESTIONS
Wheat, white, whole grain,
Italian, pugliese; any hearty,
crusty bread.

Toast with Turkey Burgers

2 TABLESPOONS OLIVE OIL

1 SMALL YELLOW ONION, FINELY CHOPPED

2 CLOVES GARLIC, MINCED

1½ POUNDS GROUND TURKEY

1 TEASPOON WORCESTERSHIRE SAUCE

3 TABLESPOONS KETCHUP

8 BREAD SLICES

SALT AND FRESHLY GROUND PEPPER

CONDIMENTS, SUCH AS KETCHUP, MUSTARD, SLICED TOMATOES, PICKLES, LETTUCE, AND SLICED RED ONION

Something from my upbringing led me to like burgers on toast rather than on a bun. Maybe it's because bread has more flavor than commercial buns. When the bread is toasted over an open flame and you've topped the burgers with plenty of ketchup, onions, lettuce, and tomatoes, you can't go wrong. I like ground turkey thigh because it is full of flavor. Sautéed onions are blended into the meat before cooking, making the burgers moist and unique.

In a small skillet over medium heat, warm the olive oil. Add the onion and cook, stirring occasionally, for about 5 minutes, or until soft. Stir in the garlic and let cool to room temperature.

In a medium bowl, combine the onion mixture, ground turkey, Worcestershire sauce, and ketchup, and divide the meat into 4 equal portions. Form each into a patty about 1 inch thick.

In a large skillet over medium heat or on a medium-hot barbecue grill, cook the burgers for 5 to 8 minutes per side.

Meanwhile, in a toaster or on the grill, toast the bread.

Season the burgers with salt and pepper to taste and place each between 2 slices of toast. Serve with your choice of condiments.

SERVES 4

MAKE-AHEAD TIP
The burgers can be made the night before and refrigerated. Then cook them when you get home from work.

BREAD SUGGESTIONS
Sourdough, wheat, white, Italian, onion, potato, focaccia, hard rolls.

Panzanella: Toasted Bread and Tomato Salad with Chicken

1 LOAF (1 POUND) CRUSTY WHITE BREAD

3 LARGE VERY RIPE TOMATOES, SEEDED, CHOPPED, AND JUICES RESERVED, OR 1 CAN (24 OUNCES) WHOLE TOMATOES, CHOPPED, JUICES RESERVED

1 RED ONION, THINLY SLICED

1 MEDIUM CUCUMBER, PEELED, HALVED, AND THINLY SLICED

1 1/2 CUPS PACKED CHOPPED FRESH BASIL

1/2 CUP EXTRA-VIRGIN OLIVE OIL

3 TABLESPOONS RED WINE VINEGAR

3 TABLESPOONS BALSAMIC VINEGAR

2 TABLESPOONS SUGAR

2 CLOVES GARLIC, MINCED

2 TABLESPOONS CAPERS

2 CUPS SKINNED AND SHREDDED COOKED CHICKEN

SALT AND FRESHLY GROUND PEPPER

I created this toasted bread salad for Muir Glen, which produces some of the finest canned organic tomatoes on the market. Although this recipe calls for fresh tomatoes, I think the canned ones work just as well because you need plenty of juices to moisten the toasted bread. Try to find the fire-roasted canned tomatoes, which add a smoky quality to the dish. Chop the tomatoes and use the juices to moisten the bread.

Preheat the oven or the toaster oven to 400 degrees F.

Using your hands, tear the bread into bite-sized pieces. Place the bread on a baking sheet and toast for 10 to 15 minutes, or until lightly browned.

Meanwhile, in a large bowl, combine the tomatoes, onion, cucumber, basil, olive oil, vinegars, sugar, garlic, capers, and chicken. Refrigerate until ready to serve.

About 15 minutes before serving, add the bread to the bowl and toss thoroughly. Season with salt and pepper to taste. Drizzle with the tomato juice to moisten the bread. If you want a very soft salad, use more juice; if you want to maintain some of the texture of the bread, use less.

SERVES 4 TO 6

MAKE-AHEAD TIP
The bread can be toasted 1 or 2 days ahead of time. The tomato, cucumber, and chicken salad can be assembled in advance and refrigerated overnight.

BREAD SUGGESTIONS
Crusty country, Italian, pugliese, herb, olive, garlic, cheese.

Toasted Polenta Corn Bread with Lamb and Apricots

1 CUP POLENTA

1 CUP UNBLEACHED ALL-PURPOSE FLOUR

1/3 CUP GRANULATED SUGAR

2 1/2 TEASPOONS BAKING POWDER

SALT

2 EGGS

1 1/2 CUPS BUTTERMILK

1/2 CUP UNSALTED BUTTER, MELTED

1 LOIN OF LAMB (ABOUT 1 1/2 POUNDS)

2 TABLESPOONS EXTRA-VIRGIN OLIVE OIL

2 CLOVES GARLIC, MINCED

FRESHLY GROUND PEPPER

6 MEDIUM FRESH APRICOTS, PITTED AND
THINLY SLICED, OR 12 DRIED APRICOT HALVES

1 1/2 TABLESPOONS CHOPPED FRESH ROSEMARY

1 TABLESPOON STONE-GROUND MUSTARD

2 ROUNDED TABLESPOONS LIGHT BROWN SUGAR

1 TABLESPOON BALSAMIC VINEGAR

1 CUP WATER OR CHICKEN BROTH

This hearty dish will warm you up on a cold winter day. I have included a simple corn bread recipe. Instead of regular cornmeal, it uses polenta, which is coarsely ground cornmeal. There are also great corn bread mixes available in most grocery stores. When push comes to shove and you are too busy to make your own, buy prebaked corn bread in the grocery store. Lamb and apricots are an aromatic and juicy topping for the toasted corn bread. Accompany with a salad of arugula tossed with olive oil, fresh mint, garlic, and balsamic vinegar.

TO MAKE THE POLENTA CORN BREAD: Preheat the oven to 375 degrees F. Generously grease a 2-quart baking pan.

In a medium bowl, stir together the polenta, flour, granulated sugar, baking powder, and a pinch of salt. In a large bowl, whisk together the eggs and buttermilk. Add the dry ingredients to the wet ingredients in three additions. Stir in the melted butter. Pour the batter into the prepared baking pan and bake for 45 minutes, or until a toothpick inserted into the center of the corn bread comes out clean. Transfer the pan to a wire rack.

Increase the oven temperature to 450 degrees F.

Rub the lamb with the olive oil and garlic, and season with salt and pepper to taste. Put the apricots, rosemary, mustard, brown sugar, and vinegar in the center of a 2-quart baking dish and mix thoroughly. Add the water. Place the lamb on top of the apricots.

continued

Bake for 30 minutes, or until the lamb is brown on the outside but still pink on the inside and an instant-read thermometer inserted into the center of the meat registers 140 degrees F. Remove from the oven and set aside.

Preheat the broiler.

Cut the corn bread into 12 slices or wedges and place on a baking sheet. Broil for 3 to 4 minutes, or until lightly browned. Transfer the corn bread to a large serving platter. Thinly slice the lamb. Spoon some of the apricots on each piece of corn bread and top with a few slices of lamb.

SERVES 4 TO 6

TIPS   Accompany the lamb with a salad of arugula tossed with olive oil, fresh mint, garlic, and balsamic vinegar.

Toasted Pepperoni Pizzas

3 TABLESPOONS OLIVE OIL

1 CLOVE GARLIC, MINCED

8 CRUSTY BREAD SLICES (EACH ABOUT 3/4 INCH THICK)

2 CUPS PREPARED TOMATO SAUCE

4 GENEROUS TABLESPOONS CHOPPED FRESH BASIL

6 OUNCES PROVOLONE CHEESE, GRATED

8 OUNCES MOZZARELLA CHEESE, GRATED

24 OR MORE TOP-QUALITY PEPPERONI SLICES

3 TABLESPOONS GRATED PARMIGIANO-REGGIANO OR ASIAGO CHEESE

What I love about this recipe is that it comes together quickly and appeals to kids as well as to grown-ups. Though delicate English muffins or crumpets are an obvious choice, I actually like these toasty pizzas even better on earthy, crusty, full-textured country bread.

Preheat the broiler.

In a small bowl, combine the olive oil and garlic. Lightly brush the bread with the garlic-infused olive oil and place on a baking sheet. Broil for 4 to 5 minutes, or until lightly browned. Remove from the broiler, but do not turn off the heat.

Using a spoon, spread a generous amount of the tomato sauce on the toasts. Sprinkle with the basil, provolone, and mozzarella. Arrange the pepperoni on top and sprinkle with the Parmigiano-Reggiano.

Broil for 4 to 5 minutes, or until the cheese is bubbly and browning. Remove from the broiler and let stand for a few minutes before diving in! Serve whole or cut into pieces.

SERVES 4

MAKE-AHEAD TIP These little pizzas can be made a day ahead, refrigerated, and cooked just before serving.

BREAD SUGGESTIONS
English muffins, crumpets, baguette, focaccia, ciabbatta, bagels, white, wheat, whole grain, Italian.

Parsley Toast with Ham and Dried Cherry Compote

6 OUNCES DRIED CHERRIES

JUICE OF 1 ORANGE (ABOUT 1/2 CUP)

JUICE OF 1 LEMON (ABOUT 1/4 CUP)

1 LARGE CINNAMON STICK, BROKEN INTO
3 PIECES

1/4 TEASPOON GROUND CLOVES

1/2 CUP SUGAR

3/4 CUP CHICKEN BROTH

2 HAM STEAKS (EACH 12 TO 16 OUNCES)

3 TABLESPOONS UNSALTED BUTTER AT ROOM
TEMPERATURE

2 TABLESPOONS CHOPPED FRESH FLAT-LEAF
PARSLEY, PLUS MORE FOR GARNISHING

4 BREAD SLICES

This dish is as American as it gets. A delicious and unusual way to enjoy toast for lunch or dinner, it's great with coleslaw or braised cabbage. You can substitute smoked chicken breasts, turkey, or tofu or smoky sausages for the ham.

In a large skillet over medium-low heat, combine the cherries, orange juice, lemon juice, cinnamon stick, cloves, and sugar. Add the broth and simmer, covered, for 15 minutes. Stir and place the ham steaks on top. Cover and simmer for 10 minutes longer. Just before serving, remove the cinnamon stick.

Meanwhile, preheat the broiler.

In a small bowl, combine the butter and the 2 tablespoons parsley. Spread the butter on the bread. Place on a baking sheet and broil for about 3 minutes, or until lightly browned.

Place 1 slice of toast on each of 4 plates. Using a large spoon, break the ham into pieces. Spoon the ham along with the cherries and juices over the toast. Garnish with parsley.

SERVES 4

BREAD SUGGESTIONS
Sourdough, white, wheat, whole grain, raisin, brioche, black.

Toast Topped with a Mushroom, Shallot, and Herb Omelette

1/4 CUP EXTRA-VIRGIN OLIVE OIL

6 SHALLOTS, THINLY SLICED

2 CLOVES GARLIC, MINCED

2 CUPS SLICED MUSHROOMS (ABOUT
6 OUNCES)

3 TABLESPOONS SWEET VERMOUTH

2 TABLESPOONS CHOPPED FRESH OREGANO,
DILL, OR MARJORAM

2 TABLESPOONS CHOPPED FRESH FLAT-LEAF
PARSLEY, PLUS MORE FOR GARNISHING

5 EGGS, BEATEN

4 TABLESPOONS SOUR CREAM OR MILK

SALT AND FRESHLY GROUND PEPPER

2 OUNCES GRUYÈRE CHEESE, GRATED

2 CRUSTY BREAD SLICES (EACH 1/2 INCH THICK)

I have always enjoyed eating breakfast foods at dinnertime, which is why I've included this recipe in the main-course chapter. When you pile the omelette on top of the toast and eat a bite of both at once, the experience in your mouth is somehow unique.

In a medium sauté pan over medium heat, warm 2 tablespoons of the olive oil. Add the shallots and cook, stirring occasionally, for 5 minutes, or until soft. Add the garlic and mushrooms and cook for 3 minutes more. Increase the heat to high, add the vermouth, oregano and the 2 tablespoons parsley, cook for one minute, and set aside to cool slightly.

In a medium bowl, whisk together the eggs and sour cream. Season with salt and pepper to taste. Using a slotted spoon, transfer the mushroom mixture to the bowl with the eggs, reserving any juices in the pan, and stir to combine.

Set the pan used to cook the mushrooms over medium heat. Add a little more olive oil if needed to prevent the egg mixture from sticking. Add the egg mixture and cook for about 5 minutes. Sprinkle half the cheese on the eggs. Cover the pan, reduce the heat to low, and cook for 3 minutes longer, or until the eggs are firm at the center.

Preheat the broiler. Brush the bread with olive oil and season lightly with salt and pepper to taste. Sprinkle with the remaining cheese. Place on a baking sheet and broil for about 3 minutes, or until the cheese is melted. Place 1 slice of toast on each of 2 plates.

When the eggs are cooked, using a spatula, loosen them from the pan and fold the omelette in half. Cut it in half and place one half on each piece of toast. Sprinkle with parsley and pepper.

SERVES 2

BREAD SUGGESTIONS
Country white, wheat, oat, whole grain, sourdough, baguette, potato, brioche, herb, chapati, black.

Sweet Toasts + Desserts

I had the most fun with this chapter. Many of the recipes will be familiar, but I added a twist, as in Toast with Blackberries and Cream Cheese (page 92), or Toast with Nut Butter, Bananas, and Chiles (page 95).

In many parts of the world, people end the meal with bread, fruit, and cheese. Why not toast that bread and serve it for dessert? Juicy ripe figs top my list of sexy foods, and they make a fabulous finish to a meal. Put them on toast with Stilton cheese and chives, and see for yourself (page 103).

I have always toasted leftover cake to warm and soften it and revitalize its freshness. In creating the recipes for this book, I discovered that toasted slices of cake have a wonderfully crispy exterior, especially the Toasted Lemon Pound Cake with Pears in Port (page 100).

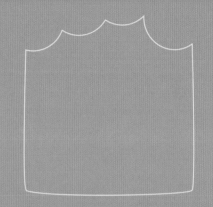

Toasted Chocolate-Espresso Cake with Warm Chocolate Sauce

1³/4 CUPS UNBLEACHED ALL-PURPOSE FLOUR

1/4 CUP INSTANT COFFEE GRANULES

1 CUP GRANULATED SUGAR

1 CUP FIRMLY PACKED LIGHT BROWN SUGAR

3/4 CUP UNSWEETENED COCOA POWDER

2 TEASPOONS BAKING POWDER

1 TEASPOON BAKING SODA

1/2 TEASPOON SALT

2 EGGS, BEATEN

3/4 CUP MILK OR SOY MILK

1/2 CUP VEGETABLE OIL

1 TEASPOON VANILLA EXTRACT

4 SQUARES SEMISWEET CHOCOLATE

2 TABLESPOONS HEAVY CREAM

Chocolate lovers will stare you straight in the eye and beg for this recipe. The warm chocolate spread on the toasted cake takes it over the top. Consider stirring a little peanut butter into the warm chocolate sauce. Or how about finishing the cake off with a scoop of espresso ice cream?

Preheat the oven to 375 degrees F. Generously oil a regular or nonstick 10-inch square baking pan. If using a regular baking pan, also line the bottom with parchment paper. You don't need to use paper for a nonstick pan.

In a medium bowl, combine the flour, coffee granules, granulated and brown sugars, cocoa powder, baking powder, baking soda, and salt and stir to mix. In another bowl, whisk or thoroughly stir together the eggs, milk, oil, and vanilla.

Gradually add the dry ingredients to the wet ingredients, stirring until completely blended; do not overmix.

Pour the batter into the prepared pan and bake for about 45 minutes, or until a toothpick inserted into the center of the cake comes out clean. Turn the pan upside down on a wire rack. Let cool for about 30 minutes, then invert and remove the cake from the pan. Let the cake cool completely, then wrap with plastic wrap and refrigerate until ready to use.

Just before serving, in a small pan over low heat or in a small bowl in the microwave, melt the chocolate. Using a fork, beat in the cream.

Cut the cake into 1-inch-thick pieces and toast. Spread the chocolate sauce on the cake and serve.

SERVES 6

MAKE-AHEAD TIP The cake keeps in the refrigerator, well wrapped, for up to 2 weeks and actually tastes even better over time.

Grandma's Healing Toast

My friend Kay Smith passed this recipe along to me from her mother, Ila. When Kay or her kids and now her grandchildren were ill, this soft, nurturing toast was nestled in their hands in lieu of chicken soup. I think it would also be good as a midnight snack. The recipe is for one since, hopefully, only one person is sick at a time. If desired, sprinkle a little cinnamon or add a touch of vanilla extract to the butter before spreading it on the bread.

Spread the butter on the bread and sprinkle with the sugar. Toast the bread in an oven or toaster oven. Cut off the crusts (a very important part of the dish, according to Kay's son, Brandon). Crumble the toast into a bowl.

In a small saucepan over medium heat, heat the milk for about 3 minutes, or until small bubbles appear around the edges of the pan and the milk is very warm to the touch. Pour the milk over the toast.

SERVES 1 SICK CHILD OF ANY AGE

1 1/2 TABLESPOONS UNSALTED BUTTER

2 WHITE BREAD SLICES

3 TEASPOONS SUGAR

1/2 CUP MILK

BREAD SUGGESTIONS
Kay's mother used store-bought white bread. English muffins, crumpets, or cinnamon-raisin bread would be delicious as well.

Sweet-Spice Cinnamon Toast

What I like best about this toasty treat is how the sugar, spices, and butter all melt together, seeping into the crevices of the toast. I find it endlessly nurturing. You can double or triple the recipe and put the spice mixture in a salt shaker with large holes. Then the mixture is ready to be sprinkled on the bread at any time. For a more luscious rendition, use cream cheese instead of butter. If you use a toaster oven, you can lighten up this recipe. Omit the butter. Toast the bread halfway, then sprinkle with the spice mixture. Return the bread to the toaster oven and toast until the sugar is warmed.

Preheat the broiler or the toaster oven.

In a small bowl, combine the sugar, cinnamon, nutmeg, and cloves. Spread the butter on the bread and sprinkle with a generous amount of the spice mixture. Place the bread on a baking sheet and broil or toast for 3 to 4 minutes, or until the butter and sugar melt.

SERVES 2

4 TABLESPOONS SUGAR

1 TEASPOON GROUND CINNAMON

$1/4$ TEASPOON FRESHLY GRATED NUTMEG

PINCH OF GROUND CLOVES

2 TABLESPOONS UNSALTED BUTTER AT ROOM TEMPERATURE

4 BREAD SLICES

BREAD SUGGESTIONS
Raisin, English muffins, crumpets, sourdough, wheat, whole grain, sweet white.

Toast with Blackberries and Cream Cheese

When blackberries are in season, I use them instead of blackberry jam on toast. Sometimes I add a little sugar, depending on the berries' natural sweetness. This recipe is one of those simple yet deliciously familiar ones that I included to remind you how easy it is to top toast with your favorite combinations. Cream cheese and jelly happens to be one of mine. Sometimes I toast individual rounds of pita bread instead of regular bread. You can substitute cherries, peaches, apricots, nectarines, or strawberries for the blackberries. The key is to use ripe, sweet fruit.

In a small bowl, mash the blackberries. Add sugar if needed. Toast the bread. Spread the cream cheese on the toast and spread the blackberries on top.

SERVES 1

$1/2$ PINT BLACKBERRIES

SUGAR, IF NEEDED

1 BREAD SLICE

$1^1/2$ TABLESPOONS CREAM CHEESE AT ROOM TEMPERATURE

BREAD SUGGESTIONS
English muffin, bagel, white, whole grain, cinnamon, brioche, baguette, pita.

Toast with Cherries and Ricotta Cheese

This light and low-fat delight is like putting a blintze on toast. It is a pleasant surprise for breakfast, brunch, or afternoon tea and makes a delicious snack. I like whole-grain toast with this topping because it adds substance, texture, and depth of flavor. Instead of cherries, use any juicy fruit, such as straw-berries, peaches, apricots, or pineapple.

In a medium bowl, combine the ³/4 cup cherries and their juices, the ricotta, and sugar to taste. Season with nutmeg and salt. Cover and refrigerate until ready to use.

Toast the bread and cut into quarters. Put the bowl of ricotta-cherry spread in the middle of a serving platter and surround with the toasts. Garnish with chopped cherries and mint.

SERVES 4 TO 6

³/4 CUP PITTED CHERRIES (FRESH OR CANNED), COARSELY CHOPPED, JUICES RESERVED, PLUS MORE FOR GARNISHING

1¹/2 CUPS RICOTTA CHEESE (WHOLE MILK OR LOW-FAT)

2 TO 4 TABLESPOONS SUGAR

PINCH OF FRESHLY GRATED NUTMEG

PINCH OF SALT

3 BREAD SLICES (EACH ABOUT ³/4 INCH THICK)

CHOPPED FRESH MINT FOR GARNISHING

BREAD SUGGESTIONS
Whole grain, wheat, crusty white, pita, crumpets, raisin, cinnamon.

Toast with Apple-Raisin Butter

1 1/2 POUNDS COOKING APPLES

1 MEDIUM CINNAMON STICK, BROKEN

3 WHOLE CLOVES

1 CUP APPLE JUICE

1 TEASPOON VANILLA EXTRACT

1/2 CUP RAISINS

2 TABLESPOONS LIGHT BROWN SUGAR

4 TO 6 BREAD SLICES

BREAD SUGGESTIONS
Apple butter is delicious on just about any bread!

At two of my restaurants, we make seasonal fruit butters to spread on our warm buttermilk biscuits and toast. Usually we use apples as the base, infusing strawberries, raspberries, or rhubarb into the butter. In the winter, when there is not much fruit available, we fold in raisins. This butter is unbeatable on toast, French toast, or smoky meats. You can make fruit butter from most firm-fleshed fruits, such as peaches, pears, apricots, and nectarines.

There are several ways to prepare the apples. I like to use a food mill because there is no need to peel or core the apples. Cut the apples into pieces and cook them with the spices until soft. Then put the mixture in the food mill, which pushes only the cooked flesh through.

If you don't use a food mill, first peel and core the apples. Cut them into pieces and cook them with the spices until soft. Then purée the mixture in a food processor or mash with a fork, which will produce a chunky butter.

Whichever method you use, in a medium saucepan over medium heat, combine the apples, cinnamon stick, cloves, and apple juice. Cook for about 20 minutes, or until the apples are very soft. Remove from the heat. Remove and discard the cinnamon stick and cloves. Mash the apples (see instructions above). Stir in the vanilla, raisins, and brown sugar. Let cool for about 20 minutes.

Toast the bread and serve with the warm apple butter. Or refrigerate the apple butter in an airtight container until ready to use. It keeps for about 1 week.

MAKES ABOUT 6 CUPS

Toast with Nut Butter, Bananas, and Chiles

4 BREAD SLICES

8 TO 12 TABLESPOONS NUT BUTTER

2 RIPE BANANAS, SLICED

2 TO 4 TABLESPOONS HONEY

1 TO 1¹/₂ TEASPOONS CHOPPED FRESH HOT RED
CHILES, OR ¹/₂ TEASPOON RED PEPPER FLAKES

In my circle of friends, this treat is an all-time favorite, bringing back memories of childhood. The blending of the chiles with sweet bananas and earthy nut butter takes it a step further, making this simple toast extraordinarily delicious.

Of course, this combination is great with good old-fashioned peanut butter, but try it with other nut butters, such as almond or walnut. I recommend buying organic nut butters for safety and quality issues, even though you may pay a little more. If you like, spread the toast with unsalted butter and then spread the nut butter on top. Utter decadence.

Toast the bread.

Spread the nut butter on the toast. Arrange the bananas on top. Drizzle with the honey and sprinkle with the chiles.

SERVES 4

BREAD SUGGESTIONS
English muffins, bagels, cinnamon, raisin, white, potato, brioche, wheat, whole grain.

Toast with Warm Sweet Balsamic Peaches

1 TABLESPOON OLIVE OIL

1/4 CUP VERY THINLY SLICED YELLOW ONION

2 MEDIUM PEACHES, PEELED, IF DESIRED,
PITTED, AND SLICED

2 TABLESPOONS FIRMLY PACKED LIGHT BROWN
SUGAR

2 TABLESPOONS BALSAMIC VINEGAR

4 BREAD SLICES (EACH 1/2 INCH THICK)

FRESHLY GROUND PEPPER

It is a cool, crisp summer morning. No work today. You know you're going to exercise later. You don't want to eat too heavily, just a snack, some fuel to get you started. This beautiful and light toast is great with coffee or, on a special occasion, with a glass of Champagne. If desired, top the peaches with ribbons of prosciutto and shaved Asiago cheese. These peaches are also wonderful spooned over chocolate ice cream or Sweet-Spice Cinnamon Toast (page 91).

In a medium sauté pan over medium heat, warm the olive oil. Add the onion and cook, stirring occasionally, for about 5 minutes. Add the peaches and brown sugar and cook, stirring occasionally, for 2 minutes longer, or until the peaches are slightly softened. Add the vinegar and stir. Cover and remove from the heat. Let stand until ready to use.

Toast the bread. Place 1 slice of toast on each of 4 plates or on a large serving platter. Spoon the warm peaches on the toast and season with pepper to taste.

SERVES 4

BREAD SUGGESTIONS
Black pepper, herb, cheese, olive, sweet white.

Toasted Honey-Walnut Cake with Cheddar and Apples

2 CUPS UNBLEACHED ALL-PURPOSE FLOUR

2 TEASPOONS BAKING POWDER

2 TEASPOONS GROUND CINNAMON

1/2 TEASPOON GROUND CLOVES

1/2 TEASPOON FRESHLY GROUND PEPPER

1 TEASPOON SALT

1 CUP (2 STICKS) UNSALTED BUTTER AT ROOM TEMPERATURE

1/2 CUP HONEY

1/2 CUP FIRMLY PACKED LIGHT BROWN SUGAR

1 CUP SOUR CREAM

1 1/2 TEASPOONS VANILLA EXTRACT

2 EGGS, BEATEN

1 1/2 CUPS (ABOUT 3 OUNCES) WALNUTS

1/2 APPLE, PEELED AND THINLY SLICED

3 OUNCES CHEDDAR CHEESE, GRATED

This basic butter cake, inspired by baker and author Beth Hensperger, is perfect for toasting. When toasted, cake that is a few days old becomes warm and soft again, almost as if it were just baked. The sweet spices and pepper add an interesting twist. The cake makes a wonderful snack, any time of day. Or serve it as a sophisticated dessert, with a glass of ruby port or vintage sherry. It is delicious even without the cheese. The cake contains enough butter so you can toast and eat it as is, with apple slices served alongside.

Preheat the oven to 375 degrees F. Generously oil a 10-inch square baking pan and line the bottom with parchment paper.

In a medium bowl, combine the flour, baking powder, cinnamon, cloves, pepper, and salt and stir to mix. In another bowl, using an electric mixer on medium-high speed, beat the butter, honey, and brown sugar until completely blended, about 1 minute. Add the sour cream, vanilla, and eggs.

Gradually add the dry ingredients to the wet ingredients, folding gently until smooth; do not overmix. Fold in the walnuts.

Pour the batter into the prepared pan and bake for about 30 minutes, or until a toothpick inserted into the center of the cake comes out clean. Transfer to a wire rack and let cool for about 30 minutes, then invert the pan and remove the cake. Let the cake cool completely, then wrap with plastic wrap and refrigerate until ready to use.

Preheat the broiler. Cut the cake into 1 1/2-inch-thick pieces and place on a baking sheet. Fan a few apple slices on top of each piece and sprinkle with the cheese. Broil for 4 to 5 minutes, or until the cheese is bubbly.

SERVES 6 TO 8

Toasted Lemon Pound Cake with Pears in Port

5 EGGS, SEPARATED

1 CUP (2 STICKS) UNSALTED BUTTER AT ROOM TEMPERATURE

1 CUP SUGAR

2 TABLESPOONS GRATED LEMON ZEST

3 TABLESPOONS FRESH LEMON JUICE

1 TABLESPOON VANILLA EXTRACT

1/4 TEASPOON SALT

2 CUPS UNBLEACHED ALL-PURPOSE FLOUR

2 FIRM COOKING PEARS (SUCH AS ANJOU, BOSC, OR SECKEL), PEELED, HALVED, AND CORED

1 CUP RUBY PORT

1 CINNAMON STICK, BROKEN INTO 2 PIECES

5 JUNIPER BERRIES

3 TABLESPOONS SUGAR

MAKE-AHEAD TIP Slice any leftover pound cake and freeze for up to 1 month. Remove from the freezer and toast when needed.

This pound cake recipe is an easy adaptation of one from Madeleine Kamman's book *The New Making of a Cook.* If you don't have time to bake a pound cake, use a store-bought one.

TO MAKE THE POUND CAKE: Preheat the oven to 375 degrees F. Lightly butter and flour a loaf pan.

Using an electric mixer on medium-high speed, beat the egg whites until soft and creamy. Transfer to a clean mixing bowl. Do not clean the other bowl.

Put the butter in the bowl used to beat the egg whites. Add the egg yolks and sugar and beat on medium speed for at least 5 minutes, or until smooth and creamy. Add the lemon zest, lemon juice, vanilla, and salt and beat for 2 minutes longer.

Using a spatula, gently fold in the egg whites, alternating with the flour. Do not overmix or the cake will be heavy and gummy.

Pour the batter into the prepared pan and bake for about 1 hour, or until a toothpick inserted into the center of the cake comes out clean. Transfer to a wire rack and let cool for 15 minutes, then invert the pan and remove the cake. Let the cake cool completely.

TO MAKE THE PEARS IN PORT: In a medium saucepan, combine the pears, port, cinnamon stick, juniper berries, and sugar. Simmer over medium heat for about 15 minutes, or until the pears are medium-soft. Transfer the pears to a small bowl, reserving the juices in the pan. Return to the stove and simmer for 15 minutes, or until the juices are reduced by half. Remove the cinnamon stick and juniper berries.

Preheat the broiler. Cut the cake into 1 1/2-inch-thick slices and broil for 3 to 4 minutes or until lightly browned. Place the toasted cake on individual plates. Slice the pears and arrange them on top of the cake. Drizzle with the port sauce.

SERVES 4

Toast with Melon, Prosciutto, and Mint

1½ CUPS COARSELY CHOPPED MELON, SUCH AS CANTALOUPE, CRENSHAW, HONEYDEW, OR CASABA

4 TO 6 LARGE FRESH MINT LEAVES, FINELY SLICED, PLUS MORE FOR GARNISHING

1 TABLESPOON BALSAMIC VINEGAR

⅛ TEASPOON FRESHLY GROUND PEPPER

2 LIMES

SUGAR, IF NEEDED

18 BAGUETTE SLICES, OR 4 BREAD SLICES, EACH CUT INTO 4 PIECES

¼ POUND PROSCIUTTO, THINLY SLICED

In late summer, when melons are fragrant and full flavored, I can't eat enough of them. Often I pair them with crusty bread and salty meats, such as prosciutto or ham to create a dish that I enjoy as much for breakfast as I do for dessert. I like to arrange the melon-topped toasts around a wedge of double-cream Brie or ripe and pungent goat Camembert. The combination is perfect with chilled glasses of gewürztraminer or a fruity Riesling. For an elegant presentation, cut the melon into slices, wrap them with prosciutto, and arrange on a serving platter. Mix together the lime juice, mint, and pepper and sprinkle over the melon. Arrange the toasts around the melon.

In a small bowl, combine the melon, mint, vinegar, and pepper. Squeeze the juice from one lime over the melon and stir. Taste for sweetness and add sugar if needed.

Toast the bread. Spoon the melon on the toasts. Roughly arrange the prosciutto on top. Place the toasts on a large serving platter. Cut the remaining lime into wedges. Garnish the platter the lime wedges and mint.

SERVES 4 TO 6

BREAD SUGGESTIONS
Baguette, brioche, whole grain, potato, white, olive, herb.

Toast with Figs, Stilton Cheese, and Chives

4 BREAD SLICES

2 TABLESPOONS EXTRA-VIRGIN OLIVE OIL

2 TABLESPOONS CHOPPED FRESH TARRAGON

8 TO 12 VERY RIPE FIGS (DEPENDING ON SIZE)

SUGAR, IF NEEDED

4 OUNCES STILTON CHEESE

2 TABLESPOONS CHOPPED FRESH CHIVES,
PLUS MORE FOR GARNISHING

FRESHLY GROUND PEPPER

CHIVE BLOSSOMS FOR GARNISHING (OPTIONAL)

1 TABLESPOON HONEY

Figs and Stilton cheese are a combination I can't resist. One afternoon, my catering manager, Jean Cooper, and I stood in the walk-in refrigerator, talking about food. (We frequently do business in the walk-in.) As we discussed logistics, we devoured a whole basket of perfectly ripe figs, stuffing them with bits of pungent Stilton cheese. The decadence of the moment was lost on the rationalization that we were blending work with pleasure. Neither Jean nor I will ever forget that magic moment. If desired, put slices of salty ham, prosciutto, or smoked turkey on the toasts and then top with the stuffed figs.

Preheat the broiler or toaster oven.

Brush the bread with the olive oil and sprinkle with the tarragon. Place the bread on a baking sheet and broil or toast for 3 to 4 minutes, or until lightly browned.

Cut the figs in half. Taste one for sweetness and sprinkle with sugar if needed. Put a generous pinch of the cheese on each fig half. Sprinkle lightly with chives and pepper. Press the fig halves back together.

Tear the toasts into the same number of pieces as you have figs. Put a stuffed fig on top of each toast. Sprinkle with chive blossoms, if using. Drizzle with honey and garnish with chives.

SERVES 4

BREAD SUGGESTIONS
Raisin, black pepper, sweet white, sourdough, whole wheat, rosemary, olive.

Index

Table of Equivalents

The exact equivalents in the following tables have been rounded for convenience.

Liquid/Dry Measures

U.S.	METRIC
1/4 teaspoon	1.25 milliliters
1/2 teaspoon	2.5 milliliters
1 teaspoon	5 milliliters
1 tablespoon (3 teaspoons)	15 milliliters
1 fluid ounce (2 tablespoons)	30 milliliters
1/4 cup	60 milliliters
1/3 cup	80 milliliters
1/2 cup	120 milliliters
1 cup	240 milliliters
1 pint (2 cups)	480 milliliters
1 quart (4 cups, 32 ounces)	960 milliliters
1 gallon (4 quarts)	3.84 liters
1 ounce (by weight)	28 grams
1 pound	454 grams
2.2 pounds	1 kilogram

Length

U.S.	METRIC
1/8 inch	3 millimeters
1/4 inch	6 millimeters
1/2 inch	12 millimeters
1 inch	2.5 centimeters

Oven Temperature

FAHRENHEIT	CELSIUS	GAS
250	120	1/2
275	140	1
300	150	2
325	160	3
350	180	4
375	190	5
400	200	6
425	220	7
450	230	8
475	240	9
500	260	10